DWELLING
IN THE MIRROR

In the first chapter of *Through the Looking-Glass*, Alice the heroine of *Alice in Wonderland*, decides to pretend that she can get through the mirror into another world. While she is saying this to herself as she kneels on the mantelpiece:

> *"And certainly the glass was beginning to melt*
> *away, just like a bright silvery mist. In another*
> *moment Alice was through the glass, and had jumped*
> *lightly down into the Looking-glass room."*

And so the dream begins which is a self-induced illusion.

DWELLING
IN THE MIRROR

A Study of Illusions
Produced by Delusive Meditation
And How to Be Free from Them

ABBOT GEORGE BURKE
(SWAMI NIRMALANANDA GIRI)

LIGHT OF THE SPIRIT
PRESS
CEDAR CREST, NEW MEXICO

Published by

Light of the Spirit Press

lightofthespiritpress.com

Light of the Spirit Monastery

P. O. Box 1370

Cedar Crest, New Mexico 87008

ocoy.org

ISBN-13: 978-0-9985998-2-3

ISBN-10: 0-9985998-2-4

Library of Congress Control Number: 2017910881

Light of the Spirit Press, Cedar Crest, NM

1. OCC010000 BODY, MIND & SPIRIT / Mindfulness & Meditation

2. SEL031000 SELF-HELP / Personal Growth / General

3. SEL032000 SELF-HELP / Spiritual

First edition, (July 2017)

03232021

CONTENTS

PREFACE

The following is part of a blurb of (at that time) a best-selling book about a woman's supposed enlightenment:

> "One day over twelve years ago, as a young American woman living in Paris, she stepped onto a city bus and suddenly and unexpectedly found herself egoless, stripped of any sense of a personal self. Struggling for years to make sense of her mental state, she consulted therapist after therapist. Eventually, she turned to spiritual teachers, coming at last to understand that this was the egoless state, the Holy Grail of so many spiritual traditions, that elusive consciousness to which so many aspire. This book is her story,

her own account of what such a terrifying event meant to her when it crashed into her everyday life, and what it means to her now."

The book is no longer in print, but I can tell you what her experience means to her now: Nothing. Because she is dead from the brain tumor that caused it.

Over and over people have mistaken trivial and pathological conditions for enlightenment, written books, given seminars and gained a devoted following. I have encountered quite a few myself, including people who believed they were the Divine Mother, Jesus Christ, the Virgin Mary, Saint Francis of Assisi, Archangel Michael, Lucifer and assorted famous masters of the past. One called our monastery and left lengthy narratives on our answering machine about herself because, she said, she did not want to die without anyone knowing about her experiences and attainment. Another one wrote me a note that simply said: "I am the Goddess!"

I have known more than one person who believed all their dreams were revelations of truth. And I have known some that continually predicted their imminent death for decades. Others told me how enlightened they were, including the one that had whiplash from "crashing into the divine light." What did they all have in common? *They had an experience!* Not of one of them was an intentional fraud. They believed their delusions based on their experience.

When a person practices a deceptive method of meditation he may experience either groundless elation or depression. Both are very dangerous for they can result in the meditator either thinking he is absolutely perfect with nothing to attain or that he is a vile sinner. Some people have even committed suicide after a supposed spiritual experience in which they felt they had experienced how evil they were. I have known many people who practiced one of the up-and-out systems which developed in them an intensely negative attitude toward the world and themselves. This latter took the form of a deep self-cynicism that developed in time into outright self-hatred. More usual, though, are the practicers of the euphoria-producing methods who really believe they are enlightened and experiencing the perfection of the Self, even though the quality of their daily way of life disproves it completely.

When in the grips of artificial euphoria produced by erroneous meditation, the unfortunate individual feels that he has nothing to attain, that he is indeed divine and eternally perfect. He does not take into account the fact that he was in no such state just previously, nor does he consider that after some time his "bliss of the self" will vanish, leaving him just as he was before: empty.

In the infantile non-cognizance of his past or his future he is in virtually the same state as a heroin user, though he believes it is because he has transcended time and relativity. He feels perfect, complete, and exalted. It is no wonder that such meditation methods, though often touted as remedies for drug addiction, lead many of their practicers into the use of drugs in an attempt to permatize and prolong the euphoria of their meditations. Many times the dupes of false meditation can be seen slipping away from a gathering or their work, and coming back some minutes later all shiny-eyed and mellow, having had their psychic fix—just as it is with the users of euphoria-producing drugs.

Nearly all phony systems of meditation are touted as sure cures for drug use. This is not so. It is appalling the number of people who take up drugs as a result of wrong meditation practices. And very often the "saved" promoters of those methods, who testify vociferously how they were delivered from dope by them, in time revert permanently, though secretly, to drug addiction while continuing to spread the false gospel and even offering drug rehabilitation programs. A significant percent (some known by me personally) become alcoholics.

The life and mind of the practicer of false meditation eventually manifest a very real disintegration and degeneration. I say eventually, because some systems deceive their practicers by at first producing seemingly positive results—and then the decline begins. Usually, though, the euphoria produced by the meditation blinds the person to the truth about himself. Some systems distort the mind so much that the person cannot perceive his real condition at all, either inwardly or outwardly.

The type of drug known as "speed" blinds the addict to the degree that he is under the influence of the drug. Only when the effect begins to wear off does he realize how "stoned" he really was. In the same way some systems of meditation radically twist the mind and life of their adherents, plunging them into great misery and inner torment, yet they are incapable of perceiving and confronting the horror in which they dwell. Simply stopping such a practice brings some alleviation, but often the distortion and scarring produced by it will not be removed except through the healing passage of time.

Just as a drunk or drug addict can lie in the gutter, dressed in rags and covered with his own vomit and yet be "feeling great" from the physical poison he has ingested, so the practicer of wrong meditation can lie in the gutter of a degenerate life, his mind in tatters, covered with the filth of his ignorance and moral corruption and still be completely satisfied—even more, considering himself a shining light of perfection.

Since delusive meditation moves the consciousness downward and outward it obviously needs no purification to facilitate it—purification would actually hinder it. Those who deaden their consciousness—especially through meat, tobacco, alcohol, drugs (including a lot of the legal ones) and sexual indulgence—easily experience the effects of such methods, since they are continuing to experience only the lower levels of their makeup, though from a different angle. As a consequence the purveyors of such destructive meditation can boast that no discipline or sacrifice, no "giving up" of anything is needed to successfully practice their type of meditation. And they are right. Starting in the mire, they end in the mire–what need of cleansing, then?

The light of spiritual day dawns gradually and steadily as does the earthly day. And it does not vanish as does the lightning flash. But the false path often abounds in bright flashes and promises of instant enlightenment. Because of the dramatic character of such flashes of psychic lightning, the followers of those paths assure themselves that the great darkness which alternates with those flashes is insignifi-cant and not a true indicator of what is–or is not–going on with them.

Most of these unfortunate people I have described are completely unreachable with reason. They cling desperately, even hysterically, to their illusions and delusions. Yet there are those who can have an experience and realize that it really cannot be real, but a vagary of their mind. Some may not understand that on their own, but can be shown by others the truth about it. For them and those that may one day be in danger of meditation-produced delusions I have written this brief study.

PART ONE

GETTING LOST IN THE MIRROR

*"The trouble with ignorance is that it picks up
confidence as it goes along."*
Arnold H. Glasgow

Glitter, not gold

"I am not afraid of you. I love now. I loved you always. I am yours and I am my own. You have forgotten what God is. But I have found Him. I love everybody. I live everywhere. I am the flesh. I am the feeling. You are dead because your aims are death. I am the spirit. I am love. I am Nijinsky of God. I love Him, and God loves me. I am a cloud of God."

Are these the words of an enlightened soul? With a few adjustments they would bring tears to the eyes of New Age seminar junkies and would sell very well as a wall poster with a nature scene background. They could even be set to music–or at least to the sound of surf and seagulls–and sold at a profit.

But they actually are the ravings of a homicidal maniac, taken down as he sat on the floor of his padded cell in a strait jacket–a strait jacket that was needed because he would try to kill anyone who came into the cell, including his wife to whom these words were dictated and whom he regarded as a spiritual ignoramus incapable of understanding his great illumination. She had forgotten God and was dead; but he had found God and was life and love–so he was convinced. But he was wrong. He was homicidal. He was insane.

The old adage is still true: All that glitters is not gold. And all that "shines" is not light, for "if the light that is in thee be darkness, how great is that darkness!" (Matthew 6:23).

Some representative examples

1. The young yogi had spent several weeks in the Himalayan depths, enclosed in a cave of his own finding. He had left the plains of northern India and come to the abode of silence. There in his cave he had engaged in various yogic practices according to his whimsy. The result was his being overwhelmed by the surety that he had attained total enlightenment and was no longer even human, but divine. Therefore he had no reason for living.

He arose and walked out of his cave in a straight path, intending that as soon as he came to a precipice he would calmly walk over it and plunge to his death, ending a now-pointless existence. But in his march to death he passed through a meadow filled with flowers. There he sat down. After some time he seemed to feel the call of all those in the world who needed him, and decided that he would not kill himself. Rather, he would return to the plains and there share his experience with others. This he did, and became a noted and prosperous guru in both India and America.

2. About the same time another yogi was sitting in the Himalayan foothills, meditating in the total darkness of a vast cave. He had an experience of the subtle energy field of the brain that is not at all an uncommon occurrence even for beginners in meditation. Yet, concluding that he was thereby enlightened, he, too, left to become a famous and wealthy guru of East and West.

3. Also around this time a young American was meandering through Ceylon. During one of his attempts to meditate he fell asleep and saw a vivid dream image of the "eye" on a peacock feather. Since the peacock is considered a spiritually significant symbol in Hindu mythology, he inferred upon waking up ("coming out of samadhi" in his later recountings) that he was enlightened. He returned to America as a "Master" who accepted credit cards.

4. A few years later another young American was studying in northern India with Tibetan refugee lamas. After many hours of meditation he fell asleep and dreamed most

realistically that he was eating radishes. When he awoke he gave forth with a violent belch–and tasted radishes! Confident that he had now gotten all there was to get in Oriental mysticism, he immediately returned to the United States and became a spiritual figure in the early years of the New Age.

5. A successful executive secretary in Canada who was also a student of yoga led a small discussion and meditation group. At the onset of menopause she began to experience mild convulsions, fainting spells, and–on occasion–visual hallucinations whenever she would attempt to practice the breathing exercises that formed the basis of her yogic practice. Highly intelligent, she readily understood that her problem was a manifestation of hormonal imbalance and the "change of life" cycle. However, when she told her small coterie of admirers that she was planning to consult a gynecologist about the advisability of medical treatment for her disorder, she encountered a flood of protest. "Mataji! You are not fainting or having 'hot flashes.' You are entering samadhi!" "This is not menopause, it is 'entering the cloud of unknowing.'" "You are experiencing 'the Great Void!'" Nonsense prevailed over good sense, since it is more appealing to the egoic mind to be thought meta-physical than menopausal. And "Stoned Out Mama," as she herself and her followers came to call her on occasion, became a spiritual leader of the New Age.

None of the foregoing accounts have been either exaggerated or written sarcastically. They are straightforward fact. They are only a drop in the vast ocean of human minds and lives devastated by the meditation-produced delusion rife in yoga cults and guru cults, and are related here not for mockery or criticism but as a warning to the undiscriminating and unwary seeker. For one of the tests set before those who seek the gold of spiritual illumination is the offering of the "fool's gold" of egoic illusion.

Dreams within dreams

"It shall even be as when an hungry man dreameth, and, behold, he eateth; but he awaketh, and his soul is empty: or as when a thirsty man dreameth, and, behold, he drinketh; but he awaketh, and, behold, he is faint, and his soul hath appetite" (Isaiah 29:8). Did you ever dream that you woke up? Remember how frustrated you were when you discovered that you were really still asleep and dreaming? Some people have had the experience of dreaming a whole series of awakenings, in each one thinking: "Now this time I am really awake," only to find out that it was still a dream. Then after waking up they pondered long and uneasily on whether or not they were really awake at last or not.

If they are more philosophically minded, those who have such an experience may wonder if this entire mode of existence within the physical body may not also be a dream–though of longer duration than their other dreams.

Might not there be another awakening—one in which this present "reality" vanishes in the dawning of another state of consciousness altogether which they will then recognize as the true state of being awake? Perhaps it might even be possible to accomplish a series of awakenings into higher and higher degrees of consciousness until at last they can enter into the Supreme Consciousness that is God Himself, so they, too, can say with the Psalmist: "I awake and am with Thee" (Psalms 139:18).

Waking up

Spiritual masters of all ages have called those who would hear to the great awakening from which there will be no more turning back to the dreams of unreality. And the process of awakening is yoga meditation.

But what if our meditation does not result in a real awakening or escape from the maze, but results only in a delusive extension of the dream of the mind? What if we even have a series of "awakening" experiences only to ultimately find that they, too, are unreal—merely new illusions replacing old ones? That this is possible I know both from my own experience and that of others who have consulted with me and whom I have observed. How many times have you and I heard people say: "I thought I got rid of that problem a long time ago; and here it still is!"

Therefore it is not enough to take up the practice of meditation in just any form. As Buddha insisted, there must be the practice of *right* meditation. What is right meditation and what is wrong meditation? The answer is not complex. Right meditation is that which removes all illusion and shows us the truth of things in a direct, unitive manner: yoga. Wrong meditation is that which either perpetuates or creates illusions, however grand and appealing they might be. And, as I have quoted at the beginning, the trouble with ignorance is that it picks up confidence as it goes along.

Necessity and a dilemma

Those who aspire to conscious self-evolution have no choice. Meditation must be taken up and made the core of their spiritual endeavors. There is no other way. But the aspirant is immediately faced with the dilemma of choosing the method of his meditation. Eventually he is going to have to take the plunge and try one out for himself. But to help you who are a fellow traveler and pilgrim of the spirit understand the range of choices, I would like to share with you the knowledge I have gathered from my own practice of various meditational systems as well as my personal observation of others and the experiences which they confided in me. I hope my exposition will not sound too dogmatic. If it does, then please consider my motivation and grant pardon.

"The Dweller at the Threshold" is a term of Western esotericism for both the ego and its accumulated powers backed by the Cosmic Delusion or Satan. This Dweller at the Threshold has inspired many delusive systems of meditation, and we should consider them as best we can.

Before beginning, however, let me assure you that after expatiating on mistaken ways of meditation I will outline a correct way which was known to the sages of India as well as to Jesus of Nazareth who lived with those sages and learned from them. (See *The Christ of India*.) That way is universal, based on the nature of the cosmos and those who are living and evolving within it. If applied correctly and persistently it brings all to the one Goal: God.

Not meditation

Some systems will not be discussed here because they are really not meditation (dhyana) at all but are intellectual exercises (manana) involving reflections on some mental concept or affirmation. Such practices can be very helpful for some, but in the final analysis they are not meditation and will not lead to enlightenment.

There are those who think they are meditating when they are really just letting the mind run around at random or intentionally fixing it on mind-generated objects, whether thoughts, concepts, visualizations or emotions. Many such exotic forms of reflection, though called meditation, are really nothing more than autosuggestion or the pondering of intellectual or visual concepts.

Many who engage in this mind-play boast of their marvelous insights, raptures, etc., mistaking simple intellectual understanding or emotional upsurge for psychic and spiritual unfoldment. This applies to the intellectual pondering of theological or philosophical principles as well. Saint Silouan of Athos, a recently canonized Eastern Orthodox saint, insisted that intellectual theologizing and the resulting delight in its revelations is the false ego's substitute for authentic mystical experience.

Up-and-out meditation

The Kingdom of God is within, and therefore as long as the Dweller at the Threshold can keep us from getting within we have no chance whatsoever of finding it. To keep us away from the true kingdom within, there is the up-and-out school of meditation. In this school the individual is convinced that the path is to escape from the body and fly away into the astral regions, there to be entertained by endless varieties of sights and sounds, rising up higher and higher to the very gates of the Infinite. But the true masters of the spiritual life (not to mention our own inner intuition) have told us that God is not "up" or "out" there, but that God is within. Therefore, a method which will take us outward and upward is going to take us away from God. That is a fact. If we take up such a practice we will eventually find ourselves further away from God than we were before.

If we think about it we can easily see the fallacy of the up-and-out philosophy of meditation. We have gone out of our bodies and beyond this world through death or involuntary astral projection during sleep or illness many times in the course of our evolutionary peregrinations, yet it has in no way enlightened us. Every night when we go to sleep, our consciousness withdraws from the physical body into the astral body. We are experiencing the astral levels of our being when we dream. When we sleep and do not dream, our awareness has withdrawn even deeper and entered into the causal part of our makeup. Whether we sleep with or without dreaming, when we wake up in the morning we are certainly not enlightened.

Inward-outward meditation

We must penetrate to the reality that lies inward beyond all the nonsense of the mind, but the tendency of the mind to turn our awareness outward is itself an internal condition. Therefore we are going to encounter it when we attempt to withdraw our focus of consciousness into the core of our being. And when we do encounter it, we can fall into the very cruel illusion of thinking that we are entering deeper and deeper into ourselves, experiencing inner realities, when in fact we are being drawn outward into experience of our external bodies—though in a more subtle manner than we have known before. This is the second type of illusion based on the outgoing tendency of the mind. The Dweller is simply not going to give up!

In this form of meditation, since we are sitting with eyes closed and our minds somewhat stilled, as a consequence we do not realize that what we perceive during such meditation is only subtler aspects of our external "garments." And so we continue to wander aimlessly in inner illusion just as heretofore we wandered in outer illusion.

The majority of the people who meditate are trapped by the mind in this illusion which we can call the inward-outward process of meditation. Like the up-and-out type it is merely another form of wandering in the mirror-maze. Those who wander in this way often say something like this: "Whenever I sit for meditation I go so deep that I don't know anything at all." (It is called deep and dreamless sleep!) "After a while I look at the clock, and often an hour has gone by without my realizing it." The truth is that such people are caught in the negative, outgoing current of consciousness. When they sit for meditation their awareness does not go in at all, but moves outward away from their spirit, sometimes being immersed in the unconsciousness of the physical body. Unhappily, some methods taught by Indian yogis do this very thing.

A true example

To understand this trick of the mind, let me give an example from real life.

In the foothills of the Indian Himalayas, there is a group of cannibalistic sorcerers living deep in the forest. This is no mere rumor. They are very much feared in the area—so much so that they are not at all secretive about themselves. The police will not interfere with them in any way. On rare occasions they come out of the forest and take from the people living in the area anything they want, for no one will oppose them. I know of an ashram that is regularly looted by them while the guru and his disciples sit motionless and silent in terror.

These evil magicians have a terrible power. If one of them meets a person in the forest whom they decide to ritually sacrifice and eat, they fix their eyes on him, fascinate him, and completely dominate his mind. The intended victim is of course afraid and wants to get away, but is afraid to turn and run lest he be knifed in the back. So he thinks that he is backing away down the path, toward the edge of the forest and to safety, with the magician walking after him. But in reality the magician is walking backwards, drawing him further into the forest to where he will be killed. All the time the poor dupe feels he is escaping when he is actually going to his death.

Through the powers of the truly cannibalistic magician-mind, in meditation we can experience that we are turning inward when in fact our awareness is being drawn outward.

What happens in inward-outward meditation

To understand the experience of those practicing an inward-outward type of meditation, we should enumerate the basic levels of our being. They are: 1) the physical body (the manomaya kosha), 2) the biomagnetic energies (the pranamaya kosha), 3) the sensory mind (the manomaya kosha), 4) the intellect (the jnanamaya kosha), and 5) the will (anandamaya kosha). Here, then, is what generally happens in meditation to the inward-outward practitioners.

First they feel restless and must consciously calm themselves and determine to persevere. Often they set in mind how long they are going to meditate and settle down to do so. At this point they are in the will level.

Next their awareness moves outward into the intellect and they find themselves thinking various kinds of thoughts. (Some schools of meditation even encourage this, and tell people to write their thoughts down.) They may be distracting thoughts or–even worse–they may be thoughts of wisdom and inspiration. Usually they stick at this level for quite a while–even for entire meditations.

After some time they begin to see lights and forms–angels, gods, masters, astral worlds, the past and the future–and perhaps experience auditory phenomena, for their awareness has moved further outward into the sensory mind and its impressions. Now the trouble really begins. Usually the person wanders for the rest of his life in realms of alternating illusions and genuine clairvoyance–the latter rendering a false credibility to the illusions.

But if the meditator has a more abstract philosophical orientation, he may wish to go beyond the mind–and so he shall, right into the region of biomagnetism where he will seem to experience "divine darkness." In this level he experiences sensations of lightness, heaviness, expanding, shrinking, falling, rising, floating, turning, whirling, rolling, somersaulting and changing into geometric shapes–the most popular sensations being an "expansion to infinity" or "the rising of the kundalini." Since the bio-magnetic level is the seat of feeling and emotion, the meditator may also be engulfed in blind sensations of peace, joy, bliss, love, energy, exuberance, inspiration and so forth. He will not be experiencing the real states themselves but only the sensations that accompany them and are often mistaken for them.

However, another step awaits the unwary meditator, and that is absorption into the inertia of the physical body. "My mind just stops," he says. And he is right! This merging of awareness into the physical level manifests as an illusory state of "non-dual" consciousness, "transcendent, beyond all time or space or conceptualization," and is also mistaken for "Entering the Divine Darkness," "The Silence," "passing into The No Thing," the "Great Void," and "entering The Cloud of Unknowing." All of these expressions just cited are terms for true, positive states, but the inexperienced person can be fooled by the ego into accepting their counterfeits.

The next state beyond even this is that of the consciousness going one step further and becoming completely separated from the five levels, including the body. Then, having stepped out of his body, the up-and-out meditation circus begins for the meditator.

It should also be pointed out that it is not uncommon for two or more of the types of phenomena just described to be experienced simultaneously, just as in our normal state we experience the various senses at the same time. The fundamental problem in all this, as well as in many other types of meditative experience, is the mistaking of physiological-neurological phenomena for spiritual experiences.

Nothing meditation

Nothing Meditation is similar in some points to the inward-outward meditation, but it needs a separate consideration. For some reason this appeals to intellectuals, perhaps because it is usually packaged in terms of inflated generalities and magnificent but unproven metaphysical assumptions that boil down in essence to "you need do nothing nor be anything." The ego loves this, and so do those in its glittering grip. A lot of talk about emptiness, mindlessness, mindfulness, no thing and such like bedazzle both the teachers and the taught. But it still comes down to nothing. And I do mean nothing, not No Thing, which is a legitimate mystical expression, however much it is applied illegitimately in erroneous meditation systems.

Exponents of nothing meditation exhort their students to stop all thoughts, silence the mind, blank the mind and "think of nothing"–an impossibility, and not at all the same thing as not thinking of anything. Basically the idea is to sit and be blank–something that frankly seems to be the continual state of a lot of people in this world, and no enlightenment has been seen to result so far.

However they may put it, the nothing meditation people are utterly caught in the mind, otherwise they would not make such a fuss over stopping it. Though caught in it, they seem to have learned nothing of its nature, for it is the essential nature of the mind to be ever changing, restless and running towards externality and material objects. There is no such thing as a still mind, for the mind is itself the manifestation and instrument of motion and change. Many who think their mind is stilled have simply lost sight of it and moved into a denser state of negative unconsciousness.

Ultimately the non-results of nothing meditation may reveal its error. For truly, from nothing only nothing comes. But many people who practice it never realize that.

Euphoric meditation

Although we have mentioned it briefly when describing what happens as the meditator experiences the bio-magnetic level, the problem of false euphoria in meditation needs to be given more consideration. In esoteric writings from India a great deal can be found about the bliss of the Self, which is very real. But as a result the conclusion has often been drawn that if a meditation practice produces a sensation of pleasure or joyfulness it is evidence that the meditator is entering into the bliss of the Self and experiencing his true being. This, however, is a grave mistake which Buddha addressed when, in outlining the Eightfold Path, he enumerated Right Bliss. This was because delusive, euphoria-producing false yoga methods were current in the days of Buddha even as they are now.

When we take an overview of the teachings of spiritual masters we will find that they point unanimously to the single root from which all the troubles of mankind arise: ignorance. The problem is not suffering–that is only a result produced by ignorance. It is knowledge in the sense of true knowing (gnosis or jnana)–i.e., spiritual realization–that is the antidote to our situation, not bliss, even Right Bliss being a side-effect of knowing.

In actuality, very few systems of euphoric meditation are able to keep their practitioners on a perpetual high. The heights of exaltation–not to mention exultation–produced by such methods are almost always followed by equally dramatic depths of depression or doldrums.

Any system which employs violent or complex breathing exercises and long holding of the breath to over-oxygenate the blood and thus produce a "natural high" which really is totally artificial, is especially unfortunate for the practitioner believes he is contacting God or his Self, when in reality he is only experiencing an abnormal condition of the nervous system–a condition which, if continually repeated, will result in a form of the same type of neurological burnout that is produced by drug use, though usually less dramatic. (This is not written from prejudice but from personal experience and years of observation.)

Over-oxygenation may also result in the temporary stimulation of certain usually dormant centers, including pleasure centers, in the brain. This artificial stimulation then produces various psychic experiences–some real and some totally hallucinatory–which also gull the unsuspecting practitioner into believing that he is experiencing genuine unfoldment of higher consciousness.

The use of such euphoria-producing methods is not only deceptive but harmful in the long run. Neurological and psychological difficulties inevitably result from prolonged practice. Their practitioners, like their chemically-dependent counterparts, are convinced that all is well and that anyone who warns them is simply being negative, bigoted, or ignorant of "the real thing." Such is the destructive effect of both drugs and incorrect meditation practices.

What has been said in the foregoing paragraph about the euphoric practices can also be said about any system that produces "amazing experiences." Such experiences have to come from somewhere and are usually the result of the energy reserves of the body being abnormally channeled into normally inactive brain centers. This both depletes and unbalances the nervous system—and consequently the mind, and usually the body.

False non-duality

Perhaps even more spiritually virulent than the euphoric practices are those which produce in the meditator a completely false sense of non-dual or infinite consciousness. These practices seem credible to those who have read in Indian philosophical treatises about resting in the Self, in a state of pure awareness beyond all objective consciousness, having discovered one's self as the eternal subject. Those writings are based on genuine spiritual experience, but the ignorant, desirous of shortcutting the process of spiritual evolution, have devised methods which produce only an approximation of those very real and holy states of being. We can think of the meditational experiences produced by these systems as being like forgeries of great works of art. They may look right, beautiful and even ingenious, but they are not the real thing, however clever or convincing.

Just as there are methods which actually draw the awareness outward while giving the illusion of turning it inward, in the same way there are methods which actually collapse the consciousness, reducing and narrowing it down to a minimal scope, while through a kind of mirror-effect giving the illusion of expansion to infinity. The practicers of such methods become convinced that they are experiencing non-dual consciousness in which they discover themselves to be the One Existent, the Self of All. They misinterpret non-duality as a state in which nothing exists but themselves–all else being illusive projections of their consciousness. This is because they have intellectually formed a false conception of non-duality–since they have no actual experience of it–and their egoic mind follows up their mistaken conclusion with an even more mistaken false confirmation.

Nothing seems to me more awful than to plumb the depths of eternity only to find that there is nothing to be found but me. To think that I am the ultimate, that beyond me there is nothing else, is dreary to the maximum degree if not downright depressing. Those psychic sociopaths who are satisfied with believing that they are the total picture are certainly contented with that view. To travel to the farthest reaches of all existence only to find nothing there but myself would be an altogether insupportable disappointment. For those to whom such impoverishment appears as infinite wealth, there are many methods designed to produce just such a "realization," illusory as it will prove to be.

Flatland

Interestingly enough, this delusive state is described in the nineteenth century science-fiction classic *Flatland* by

Edwin A. Abbott, a brilliant Shakespearean scholar and mathematician. The book is about a two-dimensional being who is suddenly pulled up into the world of three dimensions and the difficulties he encounters upon returning to the world of two dimensions and attempting to communicate his experience. At one point his inter-dimensional guide and mentor shows him two other worlds: Lineland, where there is only one dimension, and Pointland, where there are no dimensions at all—not in the sense of the transcendence of dimensionality, which is possible and even inevitable in genuine spiritual evolution, but in the sense of a regressive shrinking of consciousness to the point of incapacity for perceiving dimensions.

Here is the account. As you read it, note how the rhapsodies of the "King" of Pointland are like the modern expositions of non-dual enlightenment through meditation that are a continuing echo of the drug explosion of the nineteen-sixties.

"During my slumber I had a dream. We were moving together toward a bright but infinitesimally small Point, to which my Master directed my attention.

"'Look yonder,'" said my Guide, "'in Flatland thou hast lived; of Lineland thou hast received a vision; thou hast soared with me to the heights of Spaceland; now, in order to complete the range of thy experience, I conduct thee downward to the lowest depth of existence, even to the realm of Pointland, the Abyss of No Dimensions.

"'Behold, yon miserable creature. That Point is a Being like ourselves, but confined to the non-dimensional Gulf. He is himself his own World, his own Universe; of any other than himself he can form no conception; he knows not Length, nor Breadth, nor Height, for he has had no experience of them; he has no cognizance even of the number Two; nor has he a thought of Plurality; for he is himself his One and All, being really Nothing. Yet mark his perfect self-contentment, and hence learn this lesson, that to be self-contented is to be vile and ignorant, and that to aspire is better than to be blindly and impotently happy. Now listen.'"

"He ceased; and there arose from the little buzzing creature a tiny, low, monotonous, but distinct tinkling, as from one of your Spaceland phonographs, from which I caught these words, 'Infinite beatitude of Existence! It is; and there is none else beside It.'

"'What,'" said I, "'does the puny creature mean by "it"?'" 'He means himself,' said the Sphere: 'have you not noticed before now, that babies and babyish people who cannot distinguish themselves from the world, speak of themselves in the Third Person? But hush!'

"'It fills all Space,'" continued the little soliloquizing Creature, "'and what It fills, It is. What It thinks, that It utters; and what It utters, that It hears; and It itself is Thinker, Utterer, Hearer, Thought, Word, Audition; it is the One, and yet the All in All. Ah, the happiness ah, the happiness of Being!'"

The spiritual deadliness of such delusion is revealed further when an attempt is made to help the King of Pointland out of his false sense of non-duality so he can truly progress in consciousness.

"'Can you not startle the little thing out of its complacency?' said I. 'Tell it what it really is, as you told me; reveal to it the narrow limitations of Pointland, and lead it up to something higher.' 'That is no easy task,' said my Master; 'try you.'"

"Hereon, raising my voice to the uttermost, I addressed the Point as follows: 'Silence, silence, contemptible Creature. You call yourself the All in All, but you are the Nothing: your so-called Universe is a mere speck in a Line, and a Line is a mere shadow as compared with—' 'Hush, hush, you have said enough,' interrupted the Sphere, 'now listen, and mark the effect of your harangue on the King of Pointland.'

"The lustre of the Monarch, who beamed more brightly then ever upon hearing my words, showed clearly that he retained his complacency; and I had hardly ceased when he took up his strain again. 'Ah, the joy, ah, the joy of Thought! What can It not achieve by thinking! Its own Thought coming to Itself, suggestive of Its disparagement, thereby to enhance Its happiness! Sweet rebellion stirred up to result in triumph! Ah, the divine creative power of the All in One! Ah, the joy, the joy of Being!'

"'You see,' said my Teacher, 'how little your words have done. So far as the Monarch understands them at all, he accepts them as his own—for he cannot conceive of any other except himself—and plumes himself upon the variety of "Its Thought" as an instance of creative Power. Let us leave this God of Pointland to the ignorant fruition of his omnipresence and omniscience: nothing that you or I can do can rescue him from his self-satisfaction.'"

Really, what more need be said? The dangers of such a counterfeit transcendence and the other illusions we have considered should be evident to those not already hopelessly deluded through such profound distortions of consciousness.

Dead end self-awareness

There are practices that are supposed to reveal our true self—and they do, partially. But they also confine us to an awareness of our finite spiritual entity, even blinding us to the fact that there is a Reality that far overreaches the boundaries of our little spirit-spark. Such methods lay a great stress on "self-realization," but fail utterly to reveal the Self of our self: God. Enabling us to transcend the limitations of relative existence, they yet do not lead us to transcendence of our limited spiritual status. They then become spiritual cages in which our consciousness ignorantly rests—like the infant in its crib, warm and snug with its thumb in its mouth, resting in perfect contentment with no thought of anything further to be gained. Indeed, the infant would consider any urging to wider horizons as an outright nuisance and a disturbing of its peace and happiness.

This unfortunate state of things is perfectly symbol-ized in the film *Labyrinth*. The goblin king has stolen an infant and hidden it in the center of a vast labyrinth. The child's sister has only a few hours in which to find her little brother–otherwise he will be in the goblin domain perma-nently. Therefore she enters the labyrinth–which is filled with mirages–seeking its center. Seeing the perseverance and courage of the girl in her attempts to rescue the child, the goblin king gives up trying to frighten or discourage her and instead attempts to trick her into taking routes that will lead her right back to the beginning of the maze. Thus she will be out of the maze and consequently out of danger and conflict–but she will still not have the baby. The goblin king is the ego, the Dweller at the Threshold, the baby is the consciousness of the spirit, and the sister is the person seeking the lost spiritual awareness.

A wrong return

When the ego sees that the individual can neither be deceived by false spiritual experience nor deflected from his inner quest, as a final ploy it tries to trick the individual into abandoning the process of evolution and expansion of consciousness and simply returning to his original state in which he existed before coming into relative existence.

Now, the very reason the spirit comes into relativity is its innate urge for transcendence of its finite state, however perfect that state might have been. (For an exposition of this see *Robe of Light*.) The entire universe, visible and invisible, is an exercise field upon which the spirit strives to develop the capacity to experience wider and deeper levels of consciousness until it gains the capacity for sharing in the infinite consciousness of God. To simply return to square one–to our original state as a pure but limited consciousness beyond time and space–is a terrible error. Why? Because our innate urge for transcendence will eventually pull us out onto the playing field once more and we will have to spend aeons again climbing up to the point from which we so foolishly jumped off.

So dramatic–indeed wondrous–is the experiencing of our true self after ages of forgetfulness that it can seem perfectly sufficient to the weary spirit. But the contentment will not last forever, even if it does continue through the brief span of a single lifetime. Ultimately the divine impulse for transcendence of finite existence will arise and submerge that satisfaction in the greater and truer discontent of infinite destiny. Far from being admirable and wise, the entering back into our original status and not pressing onward to transcendence is a supreme mistake.

Therefore the methods that return us to the experience of our real being, and stop there, can also be said to be both true and false. They are true in that they give us a real experience of who and what we essentially are–which is a remarkable thing. But they are false in that they make us think there is no other destiny for us than this. They blind us to the fact that such a return to self-awareness is really not progress but a regression if it does not move on from there. The "attainment" produced by such methods is really a grievous loss of motivation and understanding.

Deadly dissolution

There are systems of meditation that actually dissolve the connections between the individual's consciousness and the bodies through which he has been evolving. When the separation is fully effected the spirit finds itself right back where it began. And will have to start all over. A waste of life indeed.

Through the effect of such practices aeons of evolution melt away and are lost to us forever, leaving us with nothing more than an awareness of our folly and the prospect of having to go through the whole endeavor again. In other words, the more successful our application of those methods, the greater our ultimate failure.

Chills and thrills

Although we have touched on it at several points, we have not specifically considered what can be called the chills and thrills school of meditation. This is composed of many systems whose intended effect is to provide continual diversions to their practicers in the form of exotic and impressive experiences. Sometimes psychic powers are also imparted to the meditator, for when the Dweller sees that the seeker is not going to be easily deflected from finding what is real, it begins to bargain with him, offering him exalted and ego-gratifying experiences, especially those that will convince him that he is enlightened or even God.

Desperate in its struggle to survive, the Dweller-ego itself promises him that he will be made a master and will inherit all powers and glories. But the price is the worst of idolatries: ego worship. Many are those who accept the hollow bargain.

To resist the terrible temptation it is necessary to understand that there is indeed but one God—and it is not "me." Those who turn away from such egoic allurements will find that eventually it can be said of them as of Jesus: "Then the devil leaveth him, and, behold, angels came and ministered unto him." (Matthew 4:11).

Tantra is especially the Great Satan in this context. Instead of wandering through astral and causal worlds, the tantric wanders through his astral and causal bodies to no purpose at all but delusion and bondage.

False raja yoga

Authentic raja yoga deals directly with the subtle energies of the yogi's various bodies for the purposes of both purification and development. The spirit, the fundamental consciousness, of each one of us, never changes because it transcends the relative world of continual and unavoidable change. But the vehicles of our spirit, being part of relativity, do indeed change and therefore can evolve to such a degree that they become perfect reflections of spirit and can eventually be absorbed into spirit, since everything has come from spirit ultimately. Genuine raja yoga is invaluable for this.

Unfortunately, over the centuries there have arisen in India a great deal of supposed raja yoga methods that are really purely physical, part of hatha yoga, not raja yoga at all. Some of these so-called pranayamas are breathing exercises that can be incredibly dangerous if practiced without strict supervision. Two factors cause this: violence and strain in practice and holding the breath forcibly for too long a time.

I have a copy of Swami Dayananda's book *Satyarth Prakash* in English which has a color photograph of the translator whose eyes are very bloodshot. The caption on that page says that the man died "attempting to raise the pranas into the head." He literally killed himself with strenuous breathing exercises. Whether they were intrinsically harmful or his practice was done incorrectly cannot be known. But this is known: the man is dead because of it.

Unhappily, there are people who for some reason like abusing themselves in various ways. They over-exercise, they over-fast, they over-medicate, they deprive themselves of sleep—anything in the name of discipline that will torment and ultimately harm them. This is a common manifestation of self-loathing found in both East and West. Such people eagerly take up practices that they overdo to their harm. So they are often attracted to false raja yoga.

False raja yoga is one of the classical chills and thrills systems. Some of the practices produce in its practicers low voltage irrelevant psychic experiences and useless revelations. That would be bad enough if they realized their valuelessness, but unfortunately they are convinced by such cosmic trivia that they are truly on the path to God, to the realization of their own divinity. Completely misinterpreting the unfolding panorama of psychic experiences, they sink in delusion as they rise in their own estimation.

Because it deals only with the biomagnetism (prana) of the human body, false raja yoga has only a superficial effect on the body or the mind. But since it does convey just a touch, a spark, of what the yogi should attain, it makes him think he has attained the whole. Then, in time, it will all fade away and he shall find himself utterly empty, devoid of any authentic realization and development.

If the practicer is young and vigorous the results are correspondingly strong and evident. But when the physical organism begins to lose its vitality—and its glandular potency in particular (especially the sexual glands)—the radiance of the false raja yogi fades away along with any psychic powers that may have developed through its practice. What remains is an empty husk. I do not write this idly or glibly, for I have had some decades of both personal experience and observation in this matter. In India I met more than one guru who in youth had been dynamic, whose photographs looked like gods. But when I met them they were shuffling around their ashrams dead-eyed and blank, hardly speaking. One time in Varanasi Mata Anandamayi spoke to me at length about the negative effects of false raja yoga practices specifically and told me to warn people about them.

False raja yoga creates alternating highs and depressions in its practitioners. One interesting trait they nearly all have is food obsession to some degree. Swami (Papa) Ramdas of Anandashram wrote about this effect in his autobiography.

What I have written regarding false raja yoga also applies to other systems involved in the development and use of "power" and subtle energies, including many practices which claim to deal with kundalini. There are legitimate systems of meditation in which kundalini comes into manifestation as a natural consequence without any intentional endeavor, but automatically as a side-effect. But many systems which focus obsessively on kundalini to exclusion of all else, virtually substituting it for God, wreak great harm and can even produce mental unbalance. This, too, I have witnessed.

Buzz-bombing meditation

Satirical as the title of this section may sound, it is absolutely true that there are systems of meditation whose sole appeal rests in the experiencing of buzzes and zaps—not resulting from their "power" as their practicers assume, but from the fact that they produce conflict and confusion in their neurological and psychic systems. When a person applies such practices he becomes "zonked" and disoriented, much like a drug high. Many drug users are attracted to such a "legal high," but they eventually go back to the drugs. Such practices are literally like slapping oneself in the face or beating oneself over the head with a hammer. "Wow! this stuff really packs a punch," exults the innocent victim. After a while the detrimental effects of such practices can no longer be ignored. But when the practicer consults with his instructors he is told that he is simply "going through a cleansing process" or "burning up karma." If he continues, the reward of his good faith is a definite breakdown mentally and physically—an expensive price to pay to eventually discover the facts. Alternatively, he burns out his subtle nervous system and becomes a husk—nothing made from something.

After a good deal of observance of those in the grip of thrills and chills and buzz bombing meditation, I realized that there was a very simple basis of their wowie zowie cataclysmic experiences. If I have a water hose turned on full force and I direct it through an open window there will be no disturbance or splashback. But if I it direct it onto the wall then there will be noise and a tremendous lot of water flying back all around and soaking me. In the same way, when a practice is correct, the higher energies move through the proper channels without inhibition. The energies of mistaken practices, on the other hand, produce conflict in the subtle bodies–especially in the astral "nerves" (nadis)–and splay out in all directions, causing disruption and disturbance of the nervous system very like the effects of taking drugs. The experience may be quite dramatic–but so is the ultimate negative result.

I have met Indian "yogis" without realization who "zap" people in the same way to impress them. Some wander the streets and do it for money.

Once a practicer of erroneous meditation methods told me that she had recently "ascended and crashed into the white light" and gotten a persistent headache and a stiff neck as a result! It seemed the politic thing to simply listen and not reply, but I was reminded of the time when a great American yogi-disciple of Yogananda, Warren Vickerman, was told by a woman that whenever she meditated she flew up out of her body and banged her head on the bedroom ceiling. "Lady," he said to her with great solemnity, "in that state there is no ceiling!"

Even more

Some practices directly attack the nervous system, through detrimental physical practices such as over-oxygenation or under-oxygenation. Some are more subtle, such as the recitations of mantras that have a negative effect on the subtle and gross bodies, especially the brain. This often occurs when the teacher dispenses bija (single syllable) mantras in hopes that the student will not discover their Hindu character—especially as invocations of gods and goddesses. Bija mantras are extremely powerful in their effect. In misapplications such as continual repetition, their effects are truly damaging. Bija mantras can wreak genuine havoc on the unsuspecting users through psychic overloading by their continual repetition. I have had much observation of this. What I am glad to tell you is that every single person who took my advice to stop repeating them experienced relief in a very short time—often in minutes.

Negative initiation

We all grew up hearing about initiation: initiation fees, initiation into college fraternities, and so forth. But in the more real world of spiritual endeavor, initiation has become an attractive and mysterious thing, although absolutely unnecessary. Essentially, initiation is the conveying of power, usually consisting of the transmission of subtle energies from one person to another by look, word or physical touch. We can think of initiation as a kind of psychic blood transfusion. And such a transfusion of energies alien to the seeker can convey great harm and sow seeds of very real psychic destruction. I have observed this in many "initiated" disciples, even being able to tell at first sight who the false guru was that had initiated them since they exhibited the same overt mental distortions of their other disciples I had met.

This is a matter of inexpressible gravity, for such a negative infusion can distort, destroy or deaden both the inner and outer bodies, causing grave damage that is not corrected by simply stopping the destructive meditation practice given along with it. For years after the cessation of a practice recognized as negative, the twisting of the inner mind can persist, often unperceived by the victim.

Here is a reliable clairvoyant's description of the psychic implantation within the aura of an initiate of one of the most popular delusive meditation systems here in the West: "A black psychic current like a thick snake comes out of the initiate's right ear and wraps down under the chin, around the neck, and then down the back and up between the legs and into the navel. Also attached to the initiate are two astral entities that look like black tennis balls. One is attached on the right shoulder at the base of the neck, and the other is at the navel. The more the initiate meditates, the bigger the 'snake' and those two entities grow and dominate his mind and life."

Fortunately, a lot of negative groups and gurus give no real initiation, but only some ineffectual rites that fool the recipient but do not flaw him. (I know of one group that claims their members become initiated "on the inner planes" when the prospective initiate receives the receipt for the initiation fee.)

Many, on the other hand, significantly alter the interior condition of their initiates, planting the seeds of distortion, anguish, illness and even madness. When these effects first make their appearance the innocent practicer is elated. "At last something that works!" he says. And it does indeed, but it works to his ultimate harm.

A terrible aspect of false meditation practice is its blinding of the aspirant to what is really going on. Through the "mirror effect" the practicer rarely becomes aware of the distortion produced by the method—much like those who take the kind of drugs known as "speed" are not even aware of the changes they produce in their minds until the drug wears off.

Negative mantras

There are mantras supposedly invoking higher beings or consciousness, as well as the Supreme Being, which really invoke and attract intelligences of the lowest and most demonic sort. This is truly horrible. Usually the groups or teachers who dispense these mantras declare that all other religions or spiritual groups than theirs are evil lies and worship evil beings. And of course the only true master on earth is their master. Anyone who observes their members with clear sight can behold the psychic ravages these frauds produce. Suicide and mental imbalance are common occurrences among them, but the cult leader and his henchmen have prepackaged explanations and rationalizations for them. I watched several of my friends begin to psychically deteriorate after becoming initiates of such groups. Fortunately, in time they all became aware of their damage and stopped the practice.

PART TWO

SYMPTOMS OF BEING IN THE MIRROR

"If it looks like a duck, quacks like a duck, walks like a duck, and swims like a duck... It's a duck!" That is so much like a joke that I think the first time we hear it we do not realize the truly good sense it embodies. It took me a long time to acknowledge that if something or someone looks, talks, acts and has the effect of something bad–such as that of a cult or false guru–then they ARE that. Simple, but hard to accustom to. So here I want to list some of the effects a negative association or practice can produce. Not that people cannot be foolish or crazy on their own, but if these symptoms arise after association with a group, person or philosophy, then there is good reason to question the wisdom of continued association and (even worse) identity.

Abnormal Sensitivity

One indication that a method of meditation is producing a pathological state in the mind is the experiencing of a high degree of sensitivity without a corresponding degree of psychological stability. Those suffering from this pathology boastfully say things like: "The experiences and insights I'm receiving in my meditations lately are so profound they are hard to bear–it's almost painful." Such persons are usually prone to violent and mercurial extremes of emotion, as well, usually without any cognizable cause or basis.

Another common form is: "I just can't bear being around Charles because I pick up so strongly on his suppressed hostility." "I can't stand going into the bank anymore–the materialistic vibrations are so intense." Sometimes noise or crowds or heavy traffic will be cited as what "nearly blows me away." And the sad part is the self-congratulatory contentment that accompanies these assertions which are really confessions of instability. This problem is usually produced by both the euphoric and the up-and-out types of meditation, but other can be the source as well.

Physical Degeneration

Though it is blithely ignored by its sufferers, one effect of wrong meditation can be physical degeneration. The terrible twisting and hypnosis of their intelligence by the mistaken methods of meditation are manifested by the meditators not only being unaware of the real character of their physical condition, but their almost frantic panegyrics on how wonderful they feel and how great their health is, and all because of their meditation. Frequently they catalog their very symptoms, declaring that their method of meditation clears up such conditions and makes them impossible.

Like many other harmful practices, many erroneous systems of meditation do not produce any negative conditions right away. Often they produce just the opposite–in the beginning. Then, when the practitioner is completely convinced of the beneficial nature of his practice, the sad dénouement begins. Yet, however much he degenerates physically or psychically, the deluded meditator is convinced it is not attributable to his practice, because in the beginning he experienced only dramatic improvements on many levels. Again we see the same tragedy of the drug addict acted out on the stage of spiritual seeking.

As already stated, sometimes the disintegrating individual does become aware of his problems. But his instructors or fellow practicers–if not he himself–assure him that he is only being "purified," "cleansed," or having his karma "speeded up." Some extreme delusionals decide that they are taking on the karma of others. (I have met some.) So he, too, congratulates himself and boasts of his supposed catharsis to whoever will listen. And continues upon the downward road.

Negative "Positivity"

The mind distorted by wrong meditation often (usually) does not perceive any defect in itself or else hysterically runs from any glimpse or hint of the truth about its dilemma, denying violently that such defects either do or even can exist. Just as some systems of meditation make the practicers over-sensitive to negativity, some destructive systems make their practicers over-sensitive to genuine positivity and create in them an outright aversion for light and an affinity for darkness. Of course, the deluded meditator sees this as just the opposite. But, as diseased eyes experience the health-giving light of the sun as painful and distressing, so these unfortunate souls come to react to simple truth.

In contrast, the sober, really positive consciousness receives any insights into its illusions with welcome and relief, uncomfortable as such insights certainly may be. Indeed, the sober person does not try to silence the voice of insight, but asks to hear more. And after hearing, acts upon it.

Fake Cosmetics

Many false meditation practices are a cosmetic that covers and hides the defects within (and even without).

One of the greatest Western occultists, Dion Fortune (Dr. Violet Firth), observed that those with genuine clairvoyance will present their psychic impressions almost apologetically, remarking that there is a chance they have misperceived or misinterpreted them. But those who are utterly deluded and have false psychic experiences adamantly and even hysterically defend them against any questioning, and bullyingly insist that others accept them as absolute truth. I well remember one of the three Jesus Christs I have met yelling at me: "You don't have any Truth Consciousness!" over and over when he asked me if I accepted he was Jesus and I said No.

Delusions of Enlightenment

People have joked for generations about those who think they are Napoleon or God, but it is no joke for those caught in such delusions—especially those self-induced through incorrect meditation. This especially applies to ego-boosting "remembering" of past lives when they supposedly were the mighty, the wise and the holy. One of my dearest friends entered a yoga cult and after a while began to announce to all that she was the reincarnation of the fake guru's guru! Eventually she joined another cult that had even crazier ideas.

Right along with these delusions are those of being enlightened. I gave some examples of this at the beginning of this study. Such delusions are of infinite variety, being custom made for each individual by his ego, so it would be impossible to describe even a fraction of them or to present a typical form of such illusion. I will, however, present one here and analyze it since we can gain some pointers from it.

A man was walking in the Himalayas looking at a panoramic view. Here is his description of what then occurred.

"What actually happened was something absurdly simple and unspectacular: just for the moment I stopped thinking. Reason and imagination and all mental chatter died down. For once, words really failed me. I forgot my name, my humanness, my thingness, all that could be called me or mine. Past and future dropped away. It was as if I had been born that instant, brand new, mindless, innocent of all memories. There existed only the Now, that present moment and what was clearly given in it. To look was enough."

Is it not wonderful how those that experience exalted states of consciousness, "beyond all mind and thought" and therefore beyond words, can so graphically and easily describe them?

Enlightenment is far beyond description. For this reason the Upanishad says: "He who tells knows it not. He who knows, tells it not." And: "If a man says 'I know,' he does not know. But if a man says 'I do not know'—perhaps he knows." This is not metaphysical gobbledegook but plain fact: "To whomsoever it is not known, to him it is known: to whomsoever it is known, he does not know.

It is not understood by those who understand it; it is understood by those who do not understand it" (Kena Upanishad 2.3). Jesus put it another way: "If I bear witness of myself, my witness is not true" (John 5:31).

But I said we would analyze this "enlightenment" account, so we should do just that.

First of all, see how many personal pronouns appear in this short paragraph. "I" occurs three times; "me" occurs twice; "my" occurs thrice; "mine" occurs once. Nine ego-indicators! These are not the marks of enlightenment. (Nor are the absurd and childish practices of referring to oneself in writing as "i" instead of "I," or referring to oneself in the third person by their name or some such circumlocution such as "this one," "this body" or simply "this.")

The terminology used is revealing. "What actually happened was something absurdly simple and unspectacular...." Enlightenment is not something that happens. It is something that *is*. The fact that the experience is something that was preceded by another state proves it is not enlightenment, for enlightenment is not an event but a recognition of what has ever been present. Therefore enlightenment by its very nature is something that cannot occur–rather it is revealed, remembered and recognized. The fact that this person speaks in this way shows that– despite claims made later on–the experience took place only within time, the abode of illusion. True enlightenment is the state of being in eternity.

"… just for the moment I stopped thinking." There you have it. "Just for the moment." It began and it ended. Enlightenment neither begins nor ends. Nor is it momentary. Nor does it have anything to do with thinking or not thinking. True, the questing soul can catch glimpses of that Light that are ephemeral, but such glimpses are no more enlightenment than a few bars of music heard from a distance are a symphony.

"Reason and imagination and all mental chatter died down." But they came back. The mind went into temporary abeyance–something that happens to all of us in dreamless sleep and under anesthesia, neither of which are gateways to enlightenment. Such a shallow and minimal event is by its nature not enlightenment.

"For once, words really failed me." Failed who? Who is telling this? The ego. Darkness.

"I forgot my name, my humanness, my thingness, all that could be called me or mine." I, I, I; my, my, my. Whose name, humanness, thingness, etc., etc.? The spirit possesses no such. Also, this is outright silly. Are we to believe that he tried to *remember* those things? If so, then it is evident that his brain was in an abnormal state akin to epilepsy, for this does happen to those in a seizure. Those who have severe migraines are very familiar with losing the ability to remember the names of those nearest them, and even of common objects. They know that the attack is lessening when the ability to recall names is once more theirs.

Furthermore, who in the state of enlightenment would stop and ask: "What is my name?" In that state we no more have a name than there is a ceiling to bang our astral heads on.

When we work at any thing that requires much attention, for that span of time we have no awareness of our name, humanness, thingness, or what is us or ours. Such concepts do not arise. Shallow self-forgetfulness of this type is common to us every day.

Once more, by the words themselves we can see that only the egoic mind is speaking.

"Past and future dropped away." From whom? They have never touched the spirit. And, as pointed out before, they returned. This is not enlightenment.

"It was as if I had been born that instant, brand new, mindless, innocent of all memories." When we are still aware of the existence or possibility of these things such as past, future, or memories, can we consider ourselves to be without them? This is not innocence, though it may be barrenness. And again: who was born, who was new? The spirit is unborn, neither new nor old. (A yogi friend of mine often said: "We need to be unborn again.") Who was receiving all these impressions and making all these evaluations?

"There existed only the Now, that present moment and what was clearly given in it." But That Which Is does not "exist." It is beyond existence, the Ground of existence.

This is why the traditions of the East (including Eastern Christianity) do not say God exists, for He is beyond either existence or non-existence. Nor could Eternity ever be spoken of as a "present moment." And of Eternity it can never truthfully be said that there is anything "in" it. Quite the opposite: It is the Great Void, the No Thing.

"To look was enough." This demonstrates that the man's senses–and therefore his body and sensory mind–were still fully functioning, and that the ego was also fully functioning, taking it all in and recording it. And aware of beginning, ending and time.

Leaving all the foregoing aside, the very fact that the writer of these words can describe his experience in terms his unenlightened readers can understand shows that his account is worthless as an exposition of enlightenment, for enlightenment is "that from which the mind and senses turn back." And that includes the intellect. Enlightenment is indescribable, the wise of all traditions have said so. Sri Ramakrishna used to say that as the jug is being filled with water there is a noise, but when it is full there is silence. So is the man of enlightenment.

This man's experience is, however, not at all incomprehensible to those who are familiar with the psychic distortion produced by drugs. I am not saying that he was on drugs, but I am saying that his experience could be either a result of past or present drug use, some abnormality of body or mind or a detrimental method of meditation–or a combination.

That he is describing a condition of the mind only is pointed out by his comment: "The fact that I happened to be walking in the Himalayas at the time probably had little to do with it; though in that country unusual states of mind are said to come more easily." States of mind are not the state of enlightenment. However, there is a kind of fever that is not uncommon in the Himalayas in which a person gets into very strange states including extreme ecstasy, wakefulness lasting for days, and disorientation which causes them to be unaware of danger and sometimes injured or killed because of it. If a person with that fever has any knowledge of yoga they are sure that they are becoming—or are—master yogis. One of my friends caught this fever and had to be taken charge of by traveling companions and forcibly hospitalized, otherwise she might died from its effects which made her believe that "at last it is happening."

This man also said that he realized he had no head. Do I need to analyze that? Certainly he lost all good sense and persisted in that state.

Mistaking Glitter For Gold

Mistaking trivial and shallow flashes such as this for enlightenment or significant spiritual experience is a symptom of wrong meditation practice. Sri Ramakrishna comes again to mind. He likened those who claim to have attained self-realization on such a flimsy basis to an ant that found a great heap of sugar. Even though only one grain filled its stomach and it could carry but one grain in its pinchers, as it went back to its nest it said to itself: "Next time I'll take the whole thing." Not likely! The old story of the frog that thought she was the biggest animal in the world also comes to mind when confronted with such claims. I once saw a *B.C.* comic strip in which a caveman climbed up a high mountain, looked in all four directions and climbed down saying: "So much for the whole world!" It is like that.

More On Enlightenment

Delusive meditation gives a delusive experience of enlightenment. It would be impossible to list and analyze their infinite variety, so we should consider some basic principles by which we can diagnose the character of the many claims to enlightenment.

First of all, anyone who claims to be enlightened is usually not. Some centuries ago a bishop learned that a great disturbance had arisen in a convent regarding a nun who was thought to be a saint by some and thought to be a fool by others. He decided to visit the convent and attempt to restore peace. Upon his arrival the nuns assembled, and without preamble the canny bishop demanded: "Which one of you is the saint?" "I am!" said a nun as she jumped up. "The matter is closed," the bishop said, turning to the abbess. "This nun is no saint, for a saint never claims to be one."

The reason a truly enlightened person does not tell others he is enlightened is the very nature of enlightenment itself. Enlightenment is not an attainment, an experience, or a state of consciousness. Rather it is the true nature of each one of us. It is not an attribute but our eternal state of being. Therefore no one can say "I have become enlightened" or "I am enlightened." The illumined simply say: "I am."

Further, being beyond time and space, enlightenment cannot really "take place."

Nor can enlightenment be in any way described, being far beyond any capability of language to convey. This being so, any verbal description of enlightenment cannot be true. And even the highest form of samadhi, nirvikalpa samadhi, is said by the yogis to be beyond describing.

The greatest exponent of spiritual reality in India, Adi Shankaracharya, in his *Stanzas on Nirvana* simply stated: "I am not bound; I am not free" for he had transcended all such possibility. That is enlightenment indeed.

The "Proof of the Pudding"...

Saint Paul claimed that on the road to Damascus he had a vision of light and spoke with the resurrected Christ. How do we know he had such an experience, and how do we know that it was real? The subsequent life of Saint Paul is the proof. In the book of Acts we see how he who began as a persecutor of Christ after his heavenly vision became himself a living image of Christ–a Christ himself.

Jesus said: "The works that I do, bear witness of me" (John 5:36). So, too, the subsequent words and deeds of both truly and falsely enlightened persons demonstrate the truth or error of their experience. We need only look at the state of mind and life of those who follow erroneous systems of meditation to discover the true character of their supposed illumination. Their claims are reminiscent of a little girl I knew who constantly sucked her thumb, except when she would take it out momentarily to boast: "I don't suck my thumb any more!" The number of people claiming enlightenment that eventually commit suicide is tragic.

The proof of the pudding is still in the living.

Why?

But why does all this happen? First, because the mind does not so easily give up its aeons-long conditioning to go outward. Second, the ego will entertain us with anything–just as long as we do not approach the Light in which it will be dissolved as the mirage it really is. Also, since from the beginning of our involvement in the relative universe we have been entertained by the "passing show," it is only to be expected that we will be susceptible to the same sort of thing on a subtler level. Only those who can cut off this deadly affinity with the passing mirage and lose the false life of the ego will be able to find the life of their spirit.

And the only way to do that is to meditate correctly and enter into our true spiritual consciousness and from there enter into union with God—or more correctly, to rediscover our union with him which has never really been disrupted except in our deluded minds.

Working Yet Failing

Just as a half-truth can be worse than an outright lie, so perhaps even worse than the deceptive methods and experiences we have so far looked at are those that do indeed accomplish exactly what they claim they do and are positive in their effects—but only to a point. These are the methods that only take us part way to the goal, only giving us a touch, a hint, of what we should attain—but that touch being so dramatic that we think we have made a great achievement when in reality we have only seen a glimmer of the wonder that can be totally experienced through correct practice of a correct method. As a result of such a mistaken satisfaction, we fail to press onward to the real heights of enlightenment.

It is possible to have real experiences but to attribute a false interpretation to them. The systems that produce these are especially precarious, since they are a mixture of reality and illusion. Those who bring them into question and analyze them will indeed find truth and reality in them and may therefore conclude that everything about them is trustworthy. Such systems are like a heap of fake and real diamonds mixed together so the false will be mistaken for the real. They are far more dangerous than those systems that are consistently false.

Of course we must not ignore the fact that many false systems do not really fool anyone at all, but rather it is the deluded egos of their adherents that gull them into following practices that a modicum of reflective intelligence would reveal as the absurdities they really are.

Emotional Manipulation

Sad as it is, I feel that I should include just one more point everyone should be wary about. A great many practicers of erroneous meditation methods are aware that their practice is somehow "off," but they keep it up because of emotional attachment to the teacher or guru, whom they believe loves them—even though they usually barely know the guru and the guru knows and cares for them not at all. This is surely the most cruel delusion of all. I have personally observed the most heartless and calculating emotional manipulation by various of the super-gurus. And I really wish to say no more on this vilest of deceptions except that this possibility should be kept in mind.

A Closing Word

To those who have patiently stayed with me during this difficult and often ugly exposition I wish to give assurance that light can dawn in even the most intense darkness. And that is the subject of the next section.

PART THREE

GETTING OUT OF THE MIRROR

How to get rid of negative initiation energies and mantras

The disillusioned initiate of an erroneous meditation system or false guru sometimes finds that his initiation has implanted within him a subtle psychic connection that he cannot break by merely discontinuing the method. This is because the implanted energy connection is tied in with the guru and the mantra he has received. Therefore he needs to rid himself of the energies of the guru and the mantra. This is done by speaking the name of the guru and the mantra aloud with the intention to transfer its energy from the initiate's life sphere.

Though you may find it strange, this method was taught to me by a great healer who also worked with healing initiates of negative gurus or groups. And through the years I have seen it work unfailingly for those who used it.

Evergreen trees (especially pine trees) have healing vibrations and one of their healing abilities is absorbing negative vibrations. Someone who has been initiated into a negative mantra can rid themselves of the negative vibrations and implants by putting all their fingertips against the needles of an evergreen or pine tree so the tips of the needles are pressing lightly against their fingertips. Then the person should clearly and carefully say aloud to the tree: "I pass on and give to you the mantra…" and repeat the mantra three times with the full intention of passing the power of the mantra into the tree… "given to me by…" and the name of the guru or his representative initiator if there was one. (An "Only True Master in the World" has to have one or more of these representatives to keep his kingdom expanding in different parts of the world. And in some yoga/guru cults the initiators claim to be representatives or "channels" of a dead guru.) If the person did not receive a mantra, but some other kind of practice or "transmission," they should say: "I give to you all the energies conveyed to me by…" and name the guru (and representative initiator if there was one). The tree will not be harmed, as it is meant to absorb negative vibrations and energies of various kinds.

It is best to do this alone so there will be no distraction.

Those who have been initiated in some way, but not into a mantra, should do the same, touching the needles as described before, but instead say: "I give to you all that is in me which has come from [here name the guru or group]" Then inhale and as you exhale, will and feel (imagine) that the influences of that guru or group are passing from you into the pine tree.

Those who have done this have found that it works.

PART FOUR

SYMPTOMS OF BEING OUT OF THE MIRROR

N ow we need to look at authentic, positive meditation practices and their effects and aspects.

Imperceptible Growth

Since the purpose of meditation is growth–evolution culminating in realization–we should remember our experience regarding our physical growth in height: we did not have any! That is, our growing up and getting taller was so natural and gradual we did not perceive it until it became evident or others pointed it out to us. In the same way, correct systems of meditation do not necessarily produce stunning, dramatic results–though they sometimes do, especially in the beginning. This is all according to the individual's karma and samskara.

But even if they do, after any initial experiences they continue to produce a harmonious unfoldment so natural that the practicer sometimes wonders if anything is happening. But eventually he perceives the very real effect. Anandamayi Ma put it this way when contrasting the chills and thrills and buzz bombing systems of meditation with correct practices: "The lightning flash comes in a moment and vividly lights up all around. Then darkness returns. But the light of day comes gradually and does not diminish."

Sobriety

We have described some methods of meditation that are illusory, but let us consider some of the effects of correct meditation.

One of the first and most important signs of correct meditation is the psychological effect that some spiritual writers have called "sobriety." Sobriety is the English translation of the Greek word *nepsis*, and is used in the sense of the direct opposite of the state of drunkenness, which involves both distortion and deadening of consciousness. Therefore a sober person sees clearly, correctly, completely and calmly. In the case of a practicer of meditation, it means that he sees both internally and externally with undistorted clarity and that he also sees fully—without any blind spots. And he is always at peace inwardly. This is especially important in relation to his view of himself and his spiritual status.

What Should Happen

Does all this mean that those who practice correct meditation simply remain flat–in "the blahs"? Not at all. The practicer of right meditation indeed does experience peace, rest, and quiet joy, but:

1. He is looking for much, much more, and never loses himself in savoring pleasurable sensations, however subtle. Never does he consider any state of mindless feelings as a spiritual experience. In fact, he ignores such experiences and keeps moving onward.

2. He never loses sight of the progress he needs to make and never falls into the error of believing he has made some great attainment in a flash. At all times he is keenly though optimistically aware of his limitations and of the very long path he still has to traverse before attaining the ultimate perfection. This is described as "discontentedly content" and "satisfied though thirsting." Both of these characteristics are produced by correct meditation itself.

The attitude of the sober practicer of right meditation toward all incidental experiences in meditation–yes, and even toward his very real attainments that are still short of the Goal–is perfectly expressed in the words of Saint

Paul: "I count not myself to have apprehended: but this one thing I do, forgetting those things which are behind, and reaching forth unto those things which are before, I press toward the mark for the prize of the high calling of God"(Philippians 3:13-14).

The high calling of God! This alone fills the horizon of him who meditates correctly. He has no time for self-savoring or self-congratulation, but presses onward to the fulfillment of that upward call.

And that is the state of sobriety.

State of mind and life: purification and perceptions of progress

Moreover, the life as well as the state of mind of the progressing meditator reveals that sobriety. This is because a sober consciousness is not afraid to look squarely at its defects and apply a remedy rather than a cosmetic. And that remedy is purification of heart and life. Therefore we can know our meditation is correct if—without becoming depressed or discouraged—we become increasingly aware of our inner defects and the need to further purify ourself to correct them.

Without the purification of all levels of our being, even the practice of correct meditation will have little or no effect. Even more, purification and refinement are needed before we can perceive the subtle effects of right meditation and to grasp the higher states of consciousness with which it puts us in touch. For this reason the fundamental scripture of yoga, the Yoga Sutras of Patanjali, prescribe ten observances or disciplines known as yama and niyama. They are:

1. Ahimsa: non-violence, non-injury, harmlessness
2. Satya: truthfulness, honesty
3. Asteya: non-stealing, honesty, non-misappropriativeness
4. Brahmacharya: sexual continence in thought, word and deed as well as control of all the senses
5. Aparigraha: non-possessiveness, non-greed, non-selfishness, non-acquisitiveness
6. Shaucha: purity, cleanliness
7. Santosha: contentment, peacefulness
8. Tapas: austerity, practical (i.e., result-producing) spiritual discipline
9. Swadhyaya: introspective self-study, spiritual study
10. Ishwarapranidhana: offering of one's life to God

Therefore one sign of correct meditation is the necessity for its practicers to cultivate purity of life and mind.

Spiritual Growth And Progress

We have already said that sobriety produces a balanced perspective regarding our present spiritual state. It also does the same in relation to spiritual progress.

Healthy physical growth is a steady though oftentimes imperceptible process. Evolution of consciousness is even subtler and longer in its duration. Any physician can bear witness to the fact that rapid growth or development in any part of the body is pathological. So, too, with meditation and spiritual advancement. Also, growth is often not perceived simply because it is natural and "makes no waves."

So what will the correct meditator experience as far as spiritual growth is concerned? It is true that he will not likely be astounded by great and rapid growth. Rather he will perceive much of his development through retrospect. That is, he may not feel the change, but when he looks back and remembers his former condition he will see a very real difference.

The Symptom of Success

Perhaps the real heart of the matter is that the one who meditates correctly becomes more and more intent on God and less and less on his own mind and feelings. The correct meditator realizes that he is an image, a mirror, of the divine perfection. Therefore any goodness that he sees in himself he correctly perceives as the goodness and perfection of God, his true Self. As he sees the image of God growing and taking shape within and without he does not attribute it to himself or to his efforts but to the love and grace of God. As he perseveres in right meditation the yogi ascends the evolutionary ladder step by step, and at each step the light is brighter. And since it is the face of God which he seeks, there is no place in his consciousness for pride or self-glorification.

In short: the meditator does not seek to be only Self-realized, but to attain God-realization–although Self-realization is a requisite for God-realization. Correct meditation fixes our awareness on God, Who is our true Self. False meditation involves the meditator more and more in his little individual self. Correct meditation makes us increasingly aware of consciousness, whereas false meditation involves us in the awareness of energy only and its manifestation as objective phenomena. This is why the enthusiasts of such systems make a big to-do about "energy," "vibrations" and "power."

Talk Should Not Be Cheap

Since "out of the abundance of the heart the mouth speaketh" (Matthew 12:34), the conversation of the true and worthy meditator will reveal a great deal about the nature of his meditative practice. If his practice is delusive, he will talk on and on about abstractions and use a lot of New Age buzzwords. If his practice is correct his words will be of practical things, or actual practice and definite principles of practice–not philosophical abstractions that sound impressive but mean nothing and have no practical application. He will not speak *about* his realization, but he will speak *from* his realization, and it will be evident. He will not thrill and chill his hearers, but will point them to the way to God-realization. And if his words are based on truth, they will be inspired to follow that way.

Also, the right meditator can distinguish between himself and God while at the same time experiencing that he and God are one. Never does he say: "I am God," any more than a wave would say: "I am the ocean." Again: whereas false meditation is used as a cosmetic to cover over spiritual defects and moral corruption with an illusory sense of perfection, correct meditation is a process of genuine purification and correction.

A Vital Point

Since the purpose of spiritual practice is to set us free, correct meditation, like correct philosophy, places the responsibility and the capacity for spiritual growth and change directly in the hands of the meditator. Always, always the meditator has freedom of choice and at every moment makes the conscious decision for higher life.

Delusive meditations cut off or anesthetize certain areas of the mind from which negativity arises and thus appear to free the meditator from problems and illusions that are in reality simply being held in abeyance only to manifest later on in either this or a future life–and usually with devastating effects on the person who thought he was free at last and spiritually transformed.

Correct meditation dispels the darkness of negativity through true illumination. Also, correct meditation often causes the meditator to confront and cope with the inner poisons which he willfully took and therefore must willfully eliminate.

If we build a brick wall of separation, we must then tear it down to end that separation. So it is with the wall of ignorance we have erected between us and God. Just as the brick wall must be dismantled brick by brick, so we must eliminate our ignorance step by step.

The Gospel of Saint John says: "But as many as received him, to them gave he power to become the sons of God" (John 1:12). It does not say that he made them sons of God, but that he gave them the power–authority and empowerment–to make themselves the children of God. That "becoming" had to be their free choice and be accomplished by their own free actions. The practicers of false meditation are always soaring and zooming, only to fall and crash. The correct meditators walk step by step, and always with full will and consciousness. They also keep quiet about it and move on ahead in private silence.

Sri Ramakrishna said: "Once, while going to the Fort, [the fort in Calcutta] I couldn't see at all that I was driving down a sloping road; but when the carriage went inside the Fort, I realized how far down I had come." And the opposite is true, as well. We do not realize how much we have progressed until we look back upon how things (especially our mind) used to be.

Right meditation is not glamorous, but it is real.

Another Ploy Of The Dweller

We must not forget as well that the Dweller at the Threshold also sometimes deludes us by getting us to incorrectly practice correct meditation. Being confident in the rightness of the system and its adherents we may not realize that our personal application is wrong or defective. Therefore a yogi should often check as to the correctness of his practice.

A friend once told me of a man who told a yoga teacher that a very simple meditation practice exhausted him. The teacher asked him to demonstrate his practice and found he was doing a ridiculous, scrambled process–not the actual technique at all. I must confess that the description of what he was doing was pretty funny, but it was not any joke for him.

It is crucial that those whose meditation practice involve a mantra make sure they are pronouncing it absolutely correctly. When I taught my friend Howard Hyde, the president of the World Bank in New Delhi, the very simple practice of Soham sadhana, I suggested that he write it down so he would not forget. He became mildly offended and assured me he would not need to write anything down, it was so simple. I understood: he was highly intelligent and used to remembering very important secular matters and plans. But in less than ten minutes he came back with pen and paper and asked me to tell him the whole thing again. So no one should be embarrassed about forgetting something in their practice. This is part of the inner shadow we all must cope with.

What is real meditation like?

Because we are exposed to the promotional hype of false meditation systems and teachers, we cannot help but be influenced, and this is especially true in the matter of what we think the practice of meditation should be like. Naturally, we hope it will be pleasant, even joyful, but the actuality is not always like that. Delusive meditation is touted as blissful, powerful, insightful, and a barrel of fun–even though it most always never really is. Real meditation is of an altogether different nature.

Before we can get to the center of the maze we have to run the whole maze. That is, before we get to the reality we have a lot of unreality to encounter–and pass by. Furthermore, the Dweller at the Threshold has no intention of giving up its domain just because we want to reclaim it for our true, divine Self.

The ego and the Dweller (they are really the same thing) have dominated us from life to life with both blandishments and threats. Although we speak of the ego as "ours," for all practical purposes we have become the possession of the ego, who is the Satan, the anti-Christ within. When we decide to turn things back around to their true order, there is going to be resistance, and often an inner war. For when we reach the level of evolution where we become conscious of our miserable state, then either the ego dies so we can get on to God or our spiritual consciousness dies so the ego can keep its domination. The two can no longer co-exist. We must choose God or ego.

Since false meditation systems in no way dislodge the ego, but enmesh us even more in the realm of illusion, the ego eagerly co-operates in their practice, urging us on and giving us experiences and thrills–even going into abeyance for a while so we can think we have conquered our inner ignorance and evil and have become pure and enlightened. But when it comes back to claim its own, it literally comes back with a vengeance and, as Jesus said, "the last state of that man is worse than the first" (Matthew 12:45; Luke 11:26). And often the worse the fallen yogi becomes the more enthusiasm he displays and the greater the spiritual claims that he makes.

In the East they often say that what is bitter in the beginning will be sweet in the end, but what is sweet in the beginning becomes bitter in the end. This is often the case with meditation systems.

We have to realize that true meditation, like true religion of which it is an integral part, is therapy not diversion. It is medicine for the sick soul. And we usually find both medicine and therapy unappealing if not downright unpleasant. It is often easy for the ego to talk us out of it, too. But those who have reached a meaningful degree of spiritual maturity go ahead and take the medicine knowing that in time it will produce health. We can say of spiritual life, and of meditation in particular, what was said about the American westward expansion: "The cowards never started and the weak died along the way."

Certainly the meditator experiences peace and quiet joy quite early in his practice, but until we get there—we are not there. So when we sit to meditate we will sometimes confront boredom, impatience, physical and mental discomfort, gripping and inane memories, fantasies, mind blather and just about anything other than peace, joy, or God. It will be more boring and annoying than painful, but for those who keep right on, caring nothing for the antics of the ego-mind, light, peace and joy come to them in the dawning of true spiritual consciousness.

What is Enlightenment Like?

What is enlightenment like? Nothing at all like what we now know. So it cannot be described. But there are experiences that indicate the dawning of real spiritual realization. They are myriad in nature, but I would like to give you an example of authentic spiritual experience that can give us quite a good idea of the basic nature of spiritual experiences that arise from correct meditation.

Saint Ambrose of Optina

The following is a written description by Saint Ambrose of Optina Monastery, in Russia, who in the nineteenth century was the spiritual guide to countless numbers of seekers in the Russian Orthodox Church. This is his own account of the experience that triggered his spiritual quest. First I will give it to you complete, and then we can analyze it together.

"It was a wonderful time in spring; and that paradise of spring, which I chose as a place of my daily visits, was the dark, thick forest. Giving myself over to this blessed state in the bosom of nature, I drank in its aromatic breath and went deeply into the spiritual apprehension of the Creator, Who is too Immense to behold.

"The surrounding world from which I came forth then retreated from me to somewhere far away and disappeared into the realm of concepts foreign to me. I was alone. Around me there was only the slumbering forest. Its ancient giants stretched far into the skies. They searched for God. I also was in search of Him.

"But suddenly, I am outside of the forest, somewhere far away, in another world, quite unknown to me, never seen by me, never imagined by me. Around me there is bright, white light! Its transcendence is so pure and enticing that I am submerged, along with my perception, into limitless depths and cannot satisfy myself with my admiration for this realm, cannot completely fill myself with its lofty spirituality. Everything is so full of beauty all around. So endearing this life—so endless the way. I am being swept across this limitless, clear space. My sight is directed upwards, does not descend anymore, does not see anything earthly. The whole of the heavenly firmament has transformed itself before me into one general bright light, pleasing to the sight.

"But I do not see the sun. I can see only its endless shining and bright light. The whole space in which I glide without hindrance, without end, without fatigue, is filled with white light, just as is its light and beautiful beings, transparent as a ray of the sun. And through them I am admiring this limitless world. The images of all these beings unknown to me are infinitely diverse and full of beauty

"I also am white and bright as they are. Over me, as over them, there reigns eternal rest. Not a single thought of mine is any longer enticed by anything earthly, not a single beat of my heart is any longer moving with human cares or earthly passion. I am all peace and rapture. But I am still moving in this infinite light, which surrounds me without change. There is nothing else in the world except for the white, bright light and these equally radiant numberless beings. But all these beings do not resemble me, nor are similar to each other; they are all endlessly varied and compellingly attractive. Amidst them, I feel myself incredibly peaceful. They evoke in me neither fear, nor amazement, nor trepidation. All that we see here does not agitate us, does not amaze us. All of us here are as if we have belonged to each other for a long time, are used to each other and are not strangers at all. We do not ask questions, we do not speak to each other about anything. We all feel and understand that there is nothing novel for us here. All our questions are solved with one glance, which sees everything and everyone. There is no trace of the wars of passions in anyone. All move in different directions, opposite to each other, not feeling any limitation, any inequality, or envy, or sorrow, or sadness. One peace reigns in all the images of entities. One light is endless for all. Oneness of life is comprehensible to all.

"My rapture at all this superseded everything. I sank into this eternal rest. No longer was my spirit disturbed by anything. And I knew nothing else earthly. None of the tribulations of my heart came to mind, even for a minute. It seemed that everything that I had experienced before on earth never existed. Such was my feeling in this new radiant world of mine. And I was at peace and joyful and desired nothing better for myself. All my earthly thoughts concerning fleeting happiness in the world died in this beautiful life, new to me, and did not come back to life again. So it seemed to me at least, there, in that better world.

"But how I came back here–I do not recall. What transitory state it was, I do not know. I only felt that I was alive, but I did not remember the world in which I lived before on earth. This did not seem at all to be a dream. Actually, about earthly things I no longer had the least notion. I only felt that the present life is mine, and that I was not a stranger in it. In this state of spirit I forgot myself and immersed myself in this light-bearing eternity. And this timelessness lasted without end, without measure, without expectation, without sleep, in this eternal rest. Thus it seemed to me that there would not be any kind of change.

"But then suddenly, the thread of my radiant life was cut off and I opened my eyes. Around me was the familiar forest, and a beam of spring sunlight was playing on its meadows. I was seized with terrible sadness. "Why am I here again?" I thought. And that radiant, light-emanating world, which I had just experienced with all its hosts of numberless visionary entities, vividly remained impressed before my mental eyes. But my physical vision did not see it any longer. This terrible and tearful sorrow I could not endure and I began to cry bitterly.

"Only after that experience I believed in the concept of the separation of soul from the body and understood what the special spiritual world was. But the question of what is the meaning of life still remained a mystery for me. And in order to penetrate into this mystery, I left this world into which I was born and embraced the monastic life."

What This Tells Us

What a thrilling narrative–a straightforward, simple and humble account of rediscovering the lost homeland of the spirit. These are the words of a saint, one whose subsequent life, rather than book sales, seminars and admirers, proved the validity of his experience. So let us look at it carefully and see what we can learn about real spiritual vision.

We have already spoken about the concept of sobriety as both a requisite and a result of correct meditation. One aspect of sobriety is the constant presence of a frame of reference that is rooted in wisdom and plain good sense. An account of an authentic spiritual experience will be pervaded with this, as well. It will also be totally lacking in the "Hey everybody! Look what happened to me! Oh, wow, wasn't it great?" kind of attitude. Such effusions are so lacking in either intelligence or meaning, they could be summed up by saying "Zip-a-dee-doo-dah!" or "Bibb-ity-Bobbity-Boo!" and letting it go at that.

This is not the case with the potential Saint Ambrose, beginner though he be. First of all, he knows his own lim-itations—as well as those of any experience he may have—for he immediately speaks of "the spiritual apprehension of the Creator, Who is too Immense to behold." He knows that however profound and astounding his experience might be, still it could be no more than a glimmering, a drop of the infinite Being that is God. He never loses sight of his eternal finitude however much he perceives God's eternal infinitude. In fact, it is that vision which convinces him of his finitude as an individual spirit within the boundless Spirit: God.

"The surrounding world from which I came forth then retreated from me to somewhere far away and disappeared into the realm of concepts foreign to me." Many of us have "forgotten the world" to some extent when out in the wilderness or desert and we do so even more every time we enter the state of dreamless sleep. But this experience is of a different order altogether. For Saint Ambrose the very concept of the world vanished from his consciousness. And it was not simply in abeyance, but became a realm "foreign" to him. The world did not simply cease to exist for him, the very ideas of existence and non-existence could no longer arise for him. This is authentic non-dual consciousness.

Yet he speaks of the forest being around him, the trees lifting high into the sky. This seems contradictory only to our linear-bound minds. He ceased to perceive the world–to even be capable of such a perception–and yet was keenly aware of it. Nothing was lost to him in that state. How this could be is simply incomprehensible. He was experiencing that of which Jesus spoke, saying: "And now, O Father, glorify thou me with thine own self with the glory which I had with thee before the world was" (John 17:5). We had this glory, too, but have lost it–even the memory of it. Saint Ambrose, one of us, was regaining it.

Saint Ambrose gained another insight. He says of the surrounding trees: "They searched for God. I also was in search of Him." He perceived that the individual consciousnesses presently inhabiting the forms of trees were dreaming that they were trees, just as he was dreaming that he was a human being. And like him they were seeking God. They (and he) were not just blindly growing toward God, subliminally evolving into to the capacity to perceive God, but from eternity in the core of their being were conscious seekers of God. In writing this there comes back to me with blessed vividness an evening in an ashram on the plains of Bengal, India. I was sitting on the veranda of the humble temple of the Lakshmanpur Yogoda Ashram with Swami Vidyananda Giri, an advanced disciple of Paramhansa Yogananda, and his friend the future Swami Bhumananda Puri. It was the time of sandhya, when day merges into evening. All things were silent–even the birds. When I commented on the stillness, Swami Bhumananda quietly said: "At these times I always think that the trees themselves are yogis, meditating on God." We were dimly intuiting it, but Saint Ambrose was seeing it.

"Seek, and ye shall find" (Matthew 7:7; Luke 11:9), Jesus assured His disciples. The questing consciousness of Saint Ambrose did indeed find, for: "Suddenly, I am outside of the forest, somewhere far away, in another world, quite unknown to me, never seen by me, never imagined by me." The dream has dissolved into a reality which had never been imagined by him, so there can be no question of autosuggestion here.

"Around me there is bright, white light!" Saint John the Beloved simply stated: "God is light" (I John 1:5), and Saint Ambrose is experiencing that. Within the infinite ocean of light that is God are contained the numberless "drops" of light that are the individual spirits, existing eternally within the Divine ocean as gods within God. Although in reality we are never separated, never changed from this status, we experience the illusions of separation and the consequent descent into material consciousness, from which we begin to evolve back toward our original state. (See *Robe of Light*.) Saint Ambrose, though caught in the web of relative existence, momentarily sees things as they are eternally in the Light of God.

Regarding this ocean of light he continues:"Its transcendence is so pure and enticing that I am submerged, along with my perception, into limitless depths and cannot satisfy myself with my admiration for this realm, cannot completely fill myself with its lofty spirituality." Those who enter into the Being of God have been described as "insatiably satisfied." This is no state of blankness or mere cessation, but an entering into Life beyond all measure or limitation whatsoever. Yet there remains the realistic awareness of the personal limitation of the individual spirit. Therefore he avers that he cannot encompass the totality of this infinite light, knowing himself as a divine part of the Divine Whole.

"Everything is so full of beauty all around. So endearing this life–so endless the way. I am being swept across this limitless, clear space. My sight is directed upwards, does not descend anymore, does not see anything earthly." By "sight"

Saint Ambrose means the orientation of his consciousness as he experiences the true Ascension of/into Christ. "The whole of the heavenly firmament has transformed itself before me into one general bright light, pleasing to the sight." Saint Bernard, centuries before, had a mystic vision in which he saw all existence gathered up into a single beam of Primal Light.

"But I do not see the sun. I can see only its endless shining and bright light." The sun of which he speaks is the metaphysical sun of Divinity. "The whole space in which I glide without hindrance, without end, without fatigue, is filled with white light, just as is its light and beautiful beings, transparent as a ray of the sun. And through them I am admiring this limitless world. The images of all these beings unknown to me are infinitely diverse and full of beauty." Thus Saint Ambrose perceives all beings as part of that ocean as well.

"I also am white and bright as they are. Over me, as over them, there reigns eternal rest." God, the Light of lights, the Spirit of spirits, is the factor which binds all these beings into one, for God is verily the ground, the source, the essence of their very existence itself.

"Not a single thought of mine is any longer enticed by anything earthly, not a single beat of my heart is any longer moving with human cares or earthly passion. I am all peace and rapture. But I am still moving in this infinite light, which surrounds me without change. There is nothing else in the world except for the white, bright light and these equally radiant numberless beings. But all these beings do not resemble me, nor are similar to each other; they are all endlessly varied and compellingly attractive." In this way he experiences the eternal diversity and distinction of all beings, for whom God alone is the common denominator.

"Amidst them, I feel myself incredibly peaceful. They evoke in me neither fear, nor amazement, nor trepidation. All that we see here does not agitate us, does not amaze us. All of us here are as if we have belonged to each other for a long time, are used to each other and are not strangers at all." This is because they have existed together eternally in the bosom of the Father, and he is rediscovering that.

"We do not ask questions, we do not speak to each other about anything. We all feel and understand that there is nothing novel for us here. All our questions are solved with one glance, which sees everything and everyone. There is no trace of the wars of passions in anyone. All move in different directions, opposite to each other, not feeling any limitation, any inequality, or envy, or sorrow, or sadness. One peace reigns in all the images of entities. One light is endless for all. Oneness of life is comprehensible to all." As stated before, this is authentic non-dual consciousness, in which God is the Unity of all.

"My rapture at all this superseded everything. I sank into this eternal rest. No longer was my spirit disturbed by anything. And I knew nothing else earthly. None of the tribulations of my heart came to mind, even for a minute. It seemed that everything that I had experienced before on earth never existed." That is true, for it was all a dream, but a dream with a purpose. "Such was my feeling in this new radiant world of mine. And I was at peace and joyful and desired nothing better for myself." He has entered into that which the yogis call Satchitananda: Existence-Knowledge-Bliss absolute. "All my earthly thoughts concerning fleeting happiness in the world died in this beautiful life, new to me, and did not come back to life again. So it seemed to me at least, there, in that better world.

"But how I came back here–I do not recall. What transitory state it was, I do not know. I only felt that I was alive, but I did not remember the world in which I lived before on earth. This did not seem at all to be a dream. Actually, about earthly things I no longer had the least notion. I only felt that the present life is mine, and that I was not a stranger in it. In this state of spirit I forgot myself and immersed myself in this light-bearing eternity. And this timelessness lasted without end, without measure, without expectation, without sleep, in this eternal rest. Thus it seemed to me that there would not be any kind of change." Exactly so.

"But then suddenly, the thread of my radiant life was cut off and I opened my eyes. Around me was the familiar forest, and a beam of spring sunlight was playing on its meadows. I was seized with terrible sadness. 'Why am I here again?' I thought. And that radiant, light-emanating world, which I had just experienced with all its hosts of numberless visionary entities, vividly remained impressed before my mental eyes. But my physical vision did not see it any longer. This terrible and tearful sorrow I could not endure and I began to cry bitterly.

"Only after that experience I believed in the concept of the separation of soul from the body and understood what the special spiritual world was. But the question of what is the meaning of life still remained a mystery for me. And in order to penetrate into this mystery, I left this world into which I was born and embraced the monastic life."

What wisdom is here! What a profound and welcome contrast to the pathological accounts given before as examples of delusions of enlightenment. Especially significant is the fact that Saint Ambrose considered this wonderful experience to be a beginning rather than an end. Instead of roaming the world giving seminars or writing books about his "enlightenment" he knew well that he had much further to go. And further he did indeed go, becoming a virtual god upon the earth, a true Master of the spiritual life. But to attain that he knew he had to do much, therefore as he so simply says: "I left this world into which I was born and embraced the monastic life" in which he was reborn irrevocably into that consciousness he has just described. And he showed the way to others, having found it himself.

PART FIVE

A RIGHT WAY OF MEDITATION

Now I would like to outline for you the most ancient and universal method of meditation: Soham Meditation.

Some history

Yoga is an eternal science intended to reveal and manifest the Eternal. Although the identity of the Supreme Self (Paramatma) and the individual Self (jivatma) with Soham is indicated in the Isha Upanishad (16) and the Brihadaranyaka Upanishad (1.4.1) respectively, no one knows exactly when it was that the knowledge of Soham Yoga was revealed in the world, but the following we do know.

A young man was wandering in the mountains somewhere in India–most likely in the Western Himalayas. He had seen no one else for a very long time, but one day he heard the faint sound of a human voice. Following it, he saw from a distance some people seated together near a river. Slipping into the water, he began swimming toward them. All along the river on that side thick reeds were growing so he was not seen as he stealthily made his way closer.

Soon he began to understand what was being said. Fascinated by the speaker's words he came as close as he dared and for a long time remained absorbed in the amazing things being spoken. For the science of yoga was being expounded by a master to his disciples. Then he heard the master say: "There is a 'fish' in the reeds over there, listening to everything I am saying. Why doesn't he come out and join us?" He did as suggested and became a resident of the master's ashram and learned both philosophy and Soham Yoga.

After diligent practice of meditation for quite some time, the master asked him to return to the plains and teach that yoga to whomever would listen. He was given a new name, Matsyendranath. (Matsyendra means Indra Among Fish and Nath means Master. Indra is king of the gods.) We have no knowledge of what the master's name was. Matsyendranath and his disciples only referred to him as Adi Nath–Original/First Master. Some believe Adi Nath was Shiva himself manifested to teach yoga, or perhaps the primeval master Bhagavan Sanatkumara about whom the Brihadaranyaka Upanishad says: "To such a one who has his stains wiped away, Bhagavan Sanatkumara shows the further shore of darkness" (7.26.2).

Matsyendra wandered throughout India, teaching those who were awakened enough to desire and comprehend the yogic path. One day in his wanderings he came to a house where the owner's wife gave him something eat and a request: that he would bless her to have a child. In response he blessed her and gave her some ashes from a sacred fire, telling her to swallow them. Then he left. The woman followed his instructions and soon conceived and gave birth to a male child. Several years later Matsyendra came there again and saw the little boy outside the house. He told him to bring his mother, and when she came he asked if she remembered him, which she did. Pointing to the boy, he said: "That is my child. I have come for him." The woman agreed and Matsyendra left with the boy whom he named Gorakhsha, Protector/Guardian of Light.

Goraksha in time became Gorakshanath–usually called Gorakhnath), the greatest yogi in India's recorded history. In every part of India there are stories told of his living in those areas. He also lived in Nepal, Tibet, Ladakh, and Bhutan. There are shrines and temples to him in all those countries, both Hindu and Buddhist. His major temple is in Gorakhpur, the birthplace of Paramhansa Yogananda whose younger brother, Sananda, was originally named Goraksha. Considering all the lore about him, Gorakhnath must have lived at least two or three hundred years, and there are many who claim that he has never left his body but is living right now in the Himalayas.

Gorakhnath had many disciples, a large number of them attaining enlightenment. They were the first members of the Nath Yogi Sampradaya, which in time numbered in its ranks the great sage Patanjali, founder of the Yoga Philosophy (Yoga Darshan) and author of the Yoga Sutras, and Jesus of Nazareth (Sri Ishanath). For many centuries the majority of monks in India were Nath Yogis, but in the nineteenth century there was a sharp decline in their numbers, which continues today. However there are several groups of "Nath Panthis" that follow the philosophy and yoga of Matsyendranath and Gorakhnath, and therefore are involved with Soham as the heart of their sadhana.

Soham

Soham means: I Am That. It is the natural vibration of the Self, which occurs spontaneously with each incoming and outgoing breath. By becoming aware of it on the conscious level by mentally repeating it in time with the breath (*So* when inhaling and *Ham* when exhaling), a yogi experiences the identity between his individual Self and the Supreme Self.

According to the Nath Yogis (see my book *Soham Yoga*) Soham has existed within the depths of God from eternity; and the same is true of every sentient being. Soham, then, will reveal our inner being. By meditating on Soham we discover our Self within which Soham has existed forever. The simple intonation of Soham in time with the breath will do everything in the unfolding of the yogi's spiritual consciousness.

The practice is very simple, and the results very profound. Truly wondrous is the fact that Soham Yoga can go on all the time, not just during meditation, if we apply ourselves to it. The whole life can become a continuous stream of liberating sadhana. "By the mantra 'Soham' separate the jivatma from the Paramatma and locate the jivatma in the heart" (Devi Bhagavatam 11.8.15).

The important thing about Soham Yoga is that it really works. It only takes perseverance.

The two oldest Upanishads on Soham

The Isha and the Brihadaranyaka are the oldest of the Upanishads, giving us the earliest record of Soham that we know.

The Isha Upanishad concludes with four mantras that are to be recited by a dying person to ensure his ascension to the solar world upon leaving his body. (These mantras are also recited by those who attend the cremation of the body.) The sixteenth mantra says: "O Pushan, the sole seer, O Controller, O Sun, offspring of Prajapati, spread forth your rays and gather up your radiant light that I may behold you of loveliest form. I am that Purusha [Spirit-Self]: I AM SOHAM" (16). (The Sanskrit text is: *Yo sav asau purushah; soham asmi.*) At the core of every sentient being Soham exists as the Self–*is* the Self. *Soham asmi* literally means "I AM THAT I AM," which is exactly what God told Moses was his Name (Exodus 3:14).

The Brihadaranyaka Upanishad (5.15.2) repeats the identical words. It earlier says: "In the beginning this (world) was only the Self [Atman], in the shape of a person. Looking around he saw nothing else than the Self. He first said, 'I am Soham [*Soham asmi*]'" (1.4.1) Thus Soham is the "first speaking" of the Absolute Itself: the expression of the knowledge and knowing of the Self. Soham is the Name (Embodiment) of the Primeval Being, the Self of the Universe and the Self of our Selfs. Soham is the Consciousness of Brahman and of the Self of each one of us. We, too, are Soham.

The ancient yogis of India discovered that the root impulse of inhalation makes the subtle sound of *So*, and the root impulse of exhalation makes the subtle sound of *Hum* (written as *Ham* in Sanskrit). Since all creation is the thought or ideation of God, meaning is inherent in everything, including the breath: "That [*So*] I am [*Ham*]." In this way every living being is perpetually intoning Soham (Sohum) at the core of their being, saying: I AM THAT: the spirit-Self which is a divine part of the Divine Infinite.

No matter how many ages we wander in forgetfulness of our divine origin and nature, we are always affirming "I am That" without ceasing at each breath. But we have lost the awareness of that sacred thread of inmost knowledge and are now wandering without direction or discernment.

But by mentally intoning Soham in time with the breath–*So* when inhaling and *Ham* when exhaling–we consciously take hold of the thread and begin moving in the right direction.

Repeating Soham in a constant flow with the breath turns the mind inward and produces spiritual awareness in an ever-increasing degree. So whenever we intone Soham in time with the breath, we align and link our consciousness with its origin: both our spirit and Divine Spirit.

For the repetition of Soham to produce its effect it must be pronounced correctly. Soham is pronounced like our English words *So* and *Hum*. The short a in Sanskrit is pronounced like the u in *up* or *hunt*, so we say "hum" even though we write it as "ham."

It is most important to pronounce the *O* correctly. It should be pronounced like the long *o* in the Italian or common American manner–as in home and lone. In England, Canada, and parts of the American South, the long *o* is sometimes pronounced as a diphthong, like two vowels jammed together: either like "*ay*-oh" or "*eh*-oh." This is not the correct manner of pronouncing the *O*, which should be a single, pure vowel sound.

The same is true of the *U* in *ham* (hum). As already pointed out, it is pronounced like the u in *up* or *hunt*–not like the u in *truth* or *push*, as is done in parts of Great Britain.

A mantra is most effective if it is mentally intoned–that is, mentally "sung"–on a single note. (The pitch does not matter–whatever is spontaneous and natural.) This makes the repetition stronger and of deeper effect, because intoning unifies the mind and naturally concentrates it.

The Practice of Soham Yoga Meditation

1. Sit upright, comfortable and relaxed, with your hands on your knees or thighs or resting, one on the other, in your lap.

2. Turn your eyes slightly downward and close them gently. This removes visual distractions and reduces your brain-wave activity by about seventy-five percent, thus helping to calm the mind. During meditation your eyes may move upward and downward naturally of their own accord. This is as it should be when it happens spontaneously. But start out with them turned slightly downward without any strain.

3. Be aware of your breath naturally (automatically) flowing in and out. Your mouth should be closed so that all breathing is done through the nose. This also aids in quieting the mind. Though your mouth is closed, the jaw muscles should be relaxed so the upper and lower teeth are not clenched or touching one another, but parted. Breathe naturally, spontaneously. Your breathing should always be easeful and natural, not deliberate or artificial.

4. Then in a very quiet and gentle manner begin *mentally* intoning Soham in time with your breathing.

(Remember: Soham is pronounced like our English words *So* and *Hum*.)

Intone *Soooooo*, prolonging a single intonation throughout each inhalation, and *Huuummm*, prolonging a single intonation throughout each exhalation, "singing" the syllables on a single note.

There is no need to pull or push the mind. Let your relaxed attention sink into and get absorbed in the mental sound of your inner intonings of Soham.

Fit the intonations to the breath—not the breath to the intonations. If the breath is short, then the intonation should be short. If the breath is long, then the intonation should be long. It does not matter if the inhalations and exhalations are not of equal length. Whatever is natural and spontaneous is what is right.

Your intonation of *Soooooo* should begin when your inhalation begins, and *Huuummm* should begin when your exhalation begins. In this way your intonations should be virtually continuous:

SooooooHuuummmSooooooHuuummmSoooooo-Huuummm.

Do not torture yourself about this—basically continuous is good enough.

5. For the rest of your meditation time keep on intoning Soham in time with your breath, calmly listening to the mental sound.

6. In Soham meditation we do not deliberately concentrate on any particular point of the body such as the third eye, as we want the subtle energies of Soham to be free to manifest themselves as is best at the moment. However, as you meditate, you may become aware of one or more areas of your brain or body at different times. This is all right when such sensations come and go spontaneously, but keep centered on your intonations of Soham in time with your breath.

7. In time your inner mental intonations of Soham may change to a more mellow or softer form, even to an inner whispering that is almost silent, but the syllables are always fully present and effective. Your intonations may even become silent, like a soundless mouthing of Soham or just the thought or movement of Soham, yet you will still be intoning Soham in your intention. And of this be sure: *Soham never ceases.* Never. You may find that your intonations of Soham move back and forth from more objective to more subtle and back to more objective. Just intone in the manner that is natural at the moment.

8. In the same way you will find that your breath will also become more subtle and refined, and slow

down. Sometimes the breath may not be perceived as movement of the lungs, but just as the subtle pranic energy movement which causes the physical breath. Your breath can even become so light that it seems as though you are not breathing at all, just *thinking* the breath (or almost so).

9. Thoughts, impressions, memories, inner sensations, and suchlike may also arise during meditation. Be calmly aware of all these things in a detached and objective manner, but keep your attention centered in your intonations of Soham in time with your breath. Do not let your attention become centered on or caught up in any inner or outer phenomena. Be calmly aware of all these things in a detached and objective manner. They are part of the transforming work of Soham, and are perfectly all right, but keep your attention centered in your intonations of Soham in time with your breath. Even though something feels very right or good when it occurs, it should not be forced or hung on to. The sum and substance of it all is this: It is not the experience we are after, but the effect. Also, since we are all different, no one can say exactly what a person's experiences in meditation are going to be like.

10. If you find yourself getting restless, distracted, fuzzy, anxious or tense in any degree, just take a

deep breath and let it out fully, feeling that you are releasing and breathing out all tensions, and continue as before.

11. Remember: Soham Yoga meditation basically consists of four things: a) sitting with the eyes closed; b) being aware of our breath as it moves in and out, and c) mentally intoning Soham in time with the breath and d) listening to those mental intonations: all in a relaxed and easeful manner, without strain.

Breath and sound are the two major spiritual powers possessed by us, so they are combined for Soham Yoga practice. It is very natural to intone Soham in time with the breathing. The way is simple and easy.

12. At the end of your meditation time, keep on intoning Soham in time with your breath as you go about your various activities, listening to the inner mantric sound, just as in meditation. One of the cardinal virtues of Soham sadhana is its capacity to be practiced throughout the day. The *Yoga Rasyanam* in verse 303 says: "Before and after the regular [meditation] practice, the repetition of Soham should be continuously done [in time with the breath] while walking, sitting or even sleeping.... This leads to ultimate success."

Can it be that simple and easy? Yes, because it goes directly to the root of our bondage which is a single–and therefore simple–thing: loss of awareness. Soham is the seed (bija) mantra of nirvanic consciousness. You take a seed, put it in the soil, water it and the sun does the rest. You plant the seed of Soham in your inner consciousness through japa and meditation and both your Self and the Supreme Self do the rest. By intentionally intoning *So* and *Ham* with the breath we are linking the conscious with superconscious mind, bringing the superconscious onto the conscious level and merging them until they become one. It is divinely simple!

Soham Yoga Sadhana in three sentences

The two supreme yogis of India's history, Matsyendranath and Gorakhnath, and the Yoga Chudamani Upanishad have made three statements that are most important for the yogi, for they present the essence of Soham Sadhana.

1. The inhalation comes in with the subtle sound of *So*, and the exhalation goes out with the subtle sound of *Ham*.
2. There is no knowledge equal to this, nor has there ever been in the past or shall be in the future any knowledge equal to this.
3. There is no japa equal to this, nor has there ever been in the past or shall be in the future any japa equal to this.

The implication is that the unequaled, and therefore supreme, knowledge and the unequaled and supreme yoga practice are the mental intonations of *So* throughout the inhalation and *Ham* throughout the exhalation. And therefore that intoning *So* and *Ham* in time with the breath is the totality of Soham Yoga practice.

Such gimmicks as thinking the breath is going up the spine with the intonation of *So* and down the spine with the intonation of *Ham*, or intoning Soham at the chakras, are not Soham Sadhana. Consequently, the Soham yogi's attention should be only on the movement of his breath and his mental intonations of *So* and *Ham* in time with it.

These three statements of Matsyendranath, Gorakhnath and the Yoga Chudamani Upanishad also imply that the difference between Soham Yoga and other yogas is the difference between lightning and lightning bugs.

How is this? Because, as we have seen in the previous chapter, according to the Isha and Brihadaranyaka Upanishads the fundamental nature of both the Supreme Self (Ishwara) and the Individual Self (Jiva) of each one of us, is Soham. Soham Sadhana takes us directly and immediately into the consciousness of the Self and the Supreme Self, simultaneously. Other yoga practices do not do this, but go about it in a roundabout manner, taking many years (if not decades) before even beginning to do what Soham Sadhana does from the very first.

In Soham Yoga only the sufficient time to experience the full range of Self-experience and become permanently established in that experience is necessary for the Soham yogi to become liberated. As soon as he truly knows: "I am Soham," the Great Work is complete. For Ishwara-pranidhana not only means offering the life to God, it also literally means offering the breath (prana) to God. This is done by intoning *So* during inhalation and *Ham* during exhalation, both in meditation and the rest of the day and night. In this way Soham Bhava, God-consciousness, is attained.

What can you expect?

Yoga and its practice is a science and the yogi is the laboratory in which that science is applied and tested. At first the aspirant takes the word of a book, a teacher or other aspirants that a yoga method is worthwhile, but eventually it is his personal experience alone that should determine his evaluation of any yoga practice. Because each person is unique in his makeup there can be a tremendous difference in each one's experience of yoga. Nevertheless, there are certain principles which can be stated.

If a yogi is especially sensitive or has practiced the method in a previous life, he may get obviously beneficial results right away. Yet for many people it takes a while for a practice to take hold and produce a steadily perceptible effect. One yogi I knew experienced satisfactory effects immediately. Then to his puzzlement for some days it seemed that absolutely nothing was happening, that his meditation was a blank. But he had the deep conviction (no doubt from a past life as a yogi) that Soham sadhana was the right and true way for him. So he kept on meditating for hours at a time. Then one morning during the final hour of meditation results began coming in the form of experiences that he had not had before. All doubt was dispelled, and he knew he was on the right track. From then onward everything was satisfactory, though there were alternating periods of active experiences and simple quiet observation of inner rest.

Experiences, as I say, can be different for everyone, but certainly peace and refinement of consciousness can be expected. Many things will occur that simply cannot be described because ordinary human language has no words for them. The real test is the yogi's state of mind outside meditation. This he should watch carefully. And he must make sure that he is always practicing correctly. Fortunately, Soham sadhana is simple and easy to do.

Warning: Do Not Interfere!

We are used to directing and controlling as much of our life as possible. But what applies to the external life as wisdom is not necessarily so in the internal life of meditation. The very simple twelve points given previously when followed exactly in a relaxed and calm manner will produce the inner environment in which Soham can do its divine work of revealing itself as the consciousness that is the yogi's true Self. If there is any interference in the form of trying to change something or direct the meditation or experience in any way, the process is interrupted and will produce no results. Naturally, since the practice is so incredibly simple and we have read all kinds of propaganda about "powerful" yogas and the chills and thrills they produce and the "profound insights" and even visions of higher worlds, etc. and etc. that supposedly result from them, we wonder if there surely isn't "more than this to it" and consider trying out such gimmicks as intoning Soham at the chakras, integrating it with some artificial form of pranayama, concentrating on the spine while visualizing/imagining currents moving up and down the spine, and other "enhancements" that may entertain but will only be obstacles to success in Soham sadhana.

The truth is that Soham intoned in time with the breath immediately begins producing a tremendous number of yogic kriyas, but kriyas that are so subtle and natural that they are usually not perceived. It takes real refinement of the mental energies to experience much of what Soham effects in the entire being of the yogi. I have been astonished at how profound the effects of Soham sadhana are, and some of my experiences have been really incredible, but I have had decades of yogic practice behind me to enable me to experience and understand the workings of Soham. I am not describing any of these experiences lest when you encounter them yourself you wonder if your experience is only autosuggestion based on my description.

Be wise and just breathe and intone Soham in time with it with eyes closed during mediation and open during the rest of the day's activity. Nothing else, but just being aware of that process and listening to the inner intonations of Soham is the secret and the assurance of success. And that is all. Soham must not be interfered with–it really cannot be, so any attempt will interrupt and spoil the practice and drag you back on the path of samsara, however "yogic" it may seem to you.

Simplicity of practice

The simpler and more easeful the yoga practice, the more deeply effective it is. This is a universal principle in the realm of inner development and experience. How is this? In the inner world of meditation things are often just the opposite to the way they are in the outer world. Whereas in the outer world a strong aggressive force is most effective in producing a change, in the inner world it is subtle, almost minimal force or movement that is most effectual–even supremely powerful. Those familiar with homeopathic medicine will understand the concept that the more subtle an element is, the more potentially effective it is. In meditation and japa the lightest touch is usually the most effective. This being so, the simple subtle intonations of Soham are the strongest and most effective form of mantric invocation.

An incident that took place during one of the crusades illustrates this. At a meeting between the leaders of the European forces and Saladin, commander of the Arab armies, one of the Europeans tried to impress and intimidate Saladin by having one of his soldiers cleave a heavy wooden chair in half with a single downstroke of his broadsword. In response, Saladin ordered someone to toss a silk scarf as light and delicate as a spider's web into the air. As it descended, he simply held his scimitar beneath it with the sharp edge upward. When the scarf touched the edge, it sheared in half and fell on either side of the blade without even a whisper as he held it completely still. This is the power of the subtle and simple practice of Soham Yoga meditation.

Subtlety of practice

Soham sadhana is extraordinarily powerful, yet until we become attuned to it by some time of practice it may seem very mild, just a kind of yogic sitting-up exercise. But it is a mighty tool of yoga alchemy. The secret of its power and effectiveness is its subtlety–the very thing that may cause it to be disregarded and not recognized for its intense value, for it is the subtle energies that are able to work lasting changes in our awareness. The more evolved consciousness or energy becomes, the more refined and subtle it becomes–truly spiritual.

It is the very subtle energies that are able to work lasting changes in our awareness. The more evolved consciousness or energy becomes, the more refined and subtle it becomes.

Thus it is the highest level of spiritual powers alone that are able to effect our ascent in consciousness.

Tension of any kind interferes with these energies. It is important, then, to keep in mind that often when things seem stuck in meditation and not moving as they should, or when the mind does not calm down, it is often because we are not relaxed sufficiently and are not allowing our inner intonations of Soham to become as subtle as they should be. For the subtler the intonations, the more effective and on target they are.

Even so, I do not mean to give you the impression that your inner intonations of Soham should become feeble or weak in the sense of becoming tenuous–only barely within your mental grasp, and liable to slip away and leave you blank. Not at all. The inner sound of the intonations may become subtler and subtler, but they do not at all become weaker–only gentler and more profound and therefore more effective.

An exception

In point 6 of the Soham Meditation instructions I said that "we do not deliberately concentrate on any particular point of the body such as the third eye, as we want the subtle energies of Soham to be free to manifest themselves as is best at the moment." There is an exception to that. On occasion, such as at the very beginning of meditation or when during the rest of the day you find your attention

DWELLING IN THE MIRROR

drifting from the breath and Soham, it can be helpful to make yourself very gently (lest you give yourself a headache from tension) aware of your entire brain (Sahasrara) area, feeling that the breath and Soham intonations are taking place there.

A short time of this awareness (which can arise spontaneously as well) is sufficient, because correct practice will result in Sahasrara awareness naturally.

And now...

And now "the way ye know" (John 14:4). However, it is always good to know as much as possible about the meaning of meditation practice and the reasons behind it as well as the purpose. Therefore I urge you to obtain and study the book *Soham Yoga, the Yoga of the Self,* which will give you a great deal of practical information on the various aspects of Soham Meditation, especially the why and wherefore of this sacred practice and the ways to apply and increase the effectiveness of your practice.

ABNORMAL STATES AND SPIRITUAL ILLUSIONS

When the brain and nervous system are in abnormal states, illusions of all kinds can occur, some of them supposedly holy and wise. But they are still illusions. Wrong meditation produces abnormal states, just as do hallucinogenic drugs. Which is why, as I have mentioned before, in the years of the Hip Era and the Yoga Boom, propagandists continually touted their meditational wares as a means to a legal high.

Here are three very interesting examples of such sincere illusions.

Dostoyevsky

The Russian writer Dostoevsky had a rare form of temporal lobe epilepsy termed "Ecstatic Epilepsy." Here is how he described his seizures."

"For several instants I experience a happiness that is impossible in an ordinary state, and of which other people have no conception. I feel full harmony in myself and in the whole world, and the feeling is so strong and sweet that for a few seconds of such bliss one could give up ten years of life, perhaps all of life. I feel that heaven descends to earth and swallows me. I really attain God and am imbued with him." This sounds quite fine, but he also recorded that his seizures were followed by intense physical and mental disturbances. It took him up to one week to recover fully from each seizure. His chief complaint was that his "head did not clear up" for several days and symptoms included, "heaviness and even pain in the head, disorders of the nerves, nervous laugh and mystical depression." Such results demonstrated the pathological nature of his experiences–of which he recorded one hundred and two.

In his novel, *The Idiot*, he relates his experiences through one of his characters, Prince Myshkin. "He was thinking, incidentally, that there was a moment or two in his epileptic condition almost before the fit itself (if it occurred in waking hours) when suddenly amid the sadness, spiritual darkness and depression, his brain seemed to catch fire at brief moments.... His sensation of being alive and his awareness increased tenfold at those moments which flashed by like lightning. His mind and heart were flooded by a dazzling light. All his agitation, doubts and worries, seemed composed in a twinkling, culminating in a great calm, full of understanding… but these moments, these glimmerings were still but a premonition of that final second (never more than a second) with which the seizure itself began. That second was, of course, unbearable." As also said before, that which begins with sweetness and ends with bitterness is negative and harmless. As Dr. Bronner's labels used to say: Judge only by the results.

Oliver Wendell Holmes

Oliver Wendell Holmes, Sr., on June 29, 1870 delivered an address before the Phi Beta Kappa Society of Harvard University that was reported in The New York Tribune, in which he related this: "I once inhaled a pretty full dose of ether, with the determination to put on record, at the earliest moment of regaining consciousness, the thought I should find uppermost in my mind. The mighty music of the triumphal march into nothingness reverberated through my brain, and filled me with a sense of infinite possibilities, which made me an archangel for the moment. The veil of eternity was lifted. The one great truth which underlies all human experience, and is the key to all the mysteries that philosophy has sought in vain to solve, flashed upon me in a sudden revelation. Henceforth all was clear: a few words had lifted my intelligence to the level of the knowledge of the cherubim. As my natural condition returned, I remembered my resolution; and, staggering to my desk, I wrote, in ill-shaped, straggling characters, the all-embracing truth still glimmering in my consciousness. The words were these: *A strong smell of turpentine prevails throughout.*"

God's message to the world…

Some time in the nineteen-fifties, a minister of the Free Methodist Church told my Aunt Eva Tabor the following.

In Peoria, Illinois, a very devout member of his church was given an anesthetic before her baby was delivered by caesarean section. When she recovered consciousness she told her husband that while she was under the anesthetic God had spoken to her given her a message for the salvation of the entire world—but upon awakening she could not remember it! For weeks this unfortunate woman prayed and racked her memory in desperation, believing that if she did not relay God's message she would be guilty of the damnation of millions. Finally her mental state was such that a psychiatrist believed that she would likely become insane. He advised that she should be given the anesthetic again to see if she could bring back the memory in that way. Since he recommended it, her physician agreed. Her husband, the minister and some close friends were with her when this was attempted. The woman vowed she would do her best to recall the message when she awoke, and the doctors asked her to speak it aloud immediately. She did so as she was coming out of the anesthetic, but when fully conscious again had no memory of the message. When she asked if she had succeeded in relaying it and what the message was, her husband silently handed her a piece of paper on which he had written it down even as she spoke it: *Bananas are a very beneficial fruit.*

DID YOU ENJOY READING THIS BOOK?

Thank you for taking the time to read *Dwelling in the Mirror*. If you enjoyed it, please consider telling your friends or posting a short review at Amazon.com, Goodreads, or the site of your choice.

Word of mouth is an author's best friend and much appreciated.

ABOUT THE AUTHOR

Abbot George Burke (Swami Nirmalananda Giri) is the founder and director of the Light of the Spirit Monastery (Atma Jyoti Ashram) in Cedar Crest, New Mexico, USA.

In his many pilgrimages to India, he had the opportunity of meeting some of India's greatest spiritual figures, including Swami Sivananda of Rishikesh and Anandamayi Ma. During his first trip to India he was made a member of the ancient Swami Order by Swami Vidyananda Giri, a direct disciple of Paramhansa Yogananda, who had himself been given sannyas by the Shankaracharya of Puri, Jagadguru Bharati Krishna Tirtha.

In the United States he also encountered various Christian saints, including Saint John Maximovich of San Francisco and Saint Philaret Voznesensky of New York. He was ordained in the Liberal Catholic Church (International) to the priesthood on January 25, 1974, and consecrated a bishop on August 23, 1975.

For many years Abbot George has researched the identity of Jesus Christ and his teachings with India and Sanatana Dharma, including Yoga. It is his conclusion that Jesus lived in India for most of his life, and was a yogi and Sanatana Dharma missionary to the West. After his resurrection he returned to India and lived the rest of his life in the Himalayas.

He has written extensively on these and other topics, many of which are posted at OCOY.org.

LIGHT OF THE SPIRIT
MONASTERY

Light of the Spirit Monastery is an esoteric Christian monastic community for those men who seek direct experience of the Spirit through meditation, sacramental worship, discipline and dedicated communal life, emphasizing the inner reality of "Christ in you the hope of glory," as taught by the illumined mystics of East and West.

The public outreach of the monastery is through its website, OCOY.org (Original Christianity and Original Yoga).There you will find many articles on Original Christianity and Original Yoga, including *Esoteric Christian Beliefs*. *Foundations of Yoga* and *How to Be a Yogi* are practical guides for anyone seriously interested in living the Yoga Life.

You will also discover many other articles on leading an effective spiritual life, including *The Yoga of the Sacraments* and *Spiritual Benefits of a Vegetarian Diet*, as well as the "Dharma for Awakening" series–in-depth commentaries on these spiritual classics: the Upanishads, the Bhagavad Gita, the Tao Teh King and the Aquarian Gospel of Jesus the Christ.

Recently added are a series of podcasts by Abbot George on meditation, the Yoga Life, and remarkable spiritual people he has met in India and elsewhere, at http://ocoy.org/podcasts/

Get your FREE Meditation Guide

Sign up for the Light of the Spirit Newsletter and get
Ten Simple Tips to Improve Your Meditation Today.

Get free updates: newsletters, blog posts, and podcasts, plus
exclusive content from Light of the Spirit Monastery.

Visit: http://ocoy.org/newsletter-registration

READING FOR AWAKENING

Light of the Spirit Press presents books on spiritual wisdom and Original Christianity and Original Yoga. From our "Dharma for Awakening" series (practical commentaries on the world's scriptures) to books on how to meditate and live a successful spiritual life, you will find books that are informative, helpful, and even entertaining.

Light of the Spirit Press is the publishing house of Light of the Spirit Monastery (Atma Jyoti Ashram) in Cedar Crest, New Mexico, USA. Our books feature the writings of the founder and director of the monastery, Abbot George Burke (Swami Nirmalananda Giri) which are also found on the monastery's website, OCOY.org.

We invite you to explore our publications in the following pages.

Find out more about our publications at

lightofthespiritpress.com

Satsang with the Abbot

Questions & Answers about Life, Spiritual Liberty, and the Pursuit of Ultimate Happiness

Grounded in the perspective of classic Indian thought, directly taught by such luminaries as Swami Sivananda of Rishikesh and Sri Anandamayi Ma, and blessed with the clarity and originality of thought that can only come from years of spiritual practice (sadhana), Abbot George Burke's answers to inquirers' questions are unique, fresh, and authoritative.

The questions in this book range from the most sublime to the most practical. "How can I attain samadhi? " "I am married with children. How can I lead a spiritual life? " "What is Self-realization?"

In Abbot George's replies to these questions the reader will discover common sense, helpful information, and a guiding light for their journey through and beyond the forest of cliches, contradictions, and confusion of yoga, Hinduism, Christianity, and metaphysical thought.

What Readers say:

"Abbot George speaks as one who knows his subject well, and answers in an manner that conveys an effortlessness and humor that puts one at ease, while, at the same time, a wisdom and sincerity which demands an attentive ear. "—*Russ Thomas*

The Unknown Lives of Jesus and Mary

Compiled from Ancient Records and Mystical Revelations

An esoteric commentary on the New Testament Apocrypha. There are historical records of the lives of Jesus Christ and his Mother Mary that have been accepted and used by the Eastern Christian Church from Apostolic times and by the Western Church until the last few centuries. They were not included in the Holy Scriptures since it could not be established beyond doubt that they were written by one of the Twelve Apostles. Yet they are of supreme value for spiritual students and those wishing to grow spiritually.

What Readers say:

"Abbot Burke elicits from every sentence in the apocryphal writings its secrets and background relevant to the spiritual path." –*Stefan Kaiser*

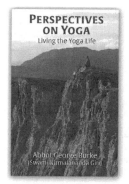

Perspectives on Yoga

Living the Yoga Life

"Dive deep; otherwise you cannot get the gems at the bottom of the ocean. You cannot pick up the gems if you only float on the surface." Sri Ramakrishna

Many people come to the joyous and liberating discovery of yoga and yoga philosophy, and then dive no deeper, resting on their first understanding of the atman, Brahman, the goal of yoga, and everything else the classic yoga philosophy teaches about "the way things are."

In *Perspectives on Yoga* author Abbot George Burke shares the gems he has found from a lifetime of "diving deep." This collection of reflections and short essays addresses the key concepts of the yoga philosophy that are so easy to take for granted.

What Readers say:

"Abbot George eloquently brings the eastern practice of seeking God inwardly to western readers who have been taught to seek God outwardly."—*Bill Braddock*

Soham Yoga
The Yoga of the Self

An in-depth guide to the practice of Soham sadhana.

Soham (which is pronounced like "Sohum") means: I Am That. It is the natural vibration of the Self, which occurs spontaneously with each incoming and outgoing breath. By becoming aware of it on the conscious level by mentally repeating it in time with the breath (*So* when inhaling and *Ham* when exhaling), a yogi experiences the identity between his individual Self and the Supreme Self.

The practice is very simple, and the results very profound. Truly wondrous is the fact that Soham Yoga can go on all the time, not just during meditation, if we apply ourselves to it. The whole life can become a continuous stream of liberating sadhana. When we repeat Soham in time with the breath we are invoking our eternal being. This is why we need only listen to our inner mental intonations of Soham in time with the breath which itself is Soham.

What Readers say:

"The more I read this book, study it and practice Soham meditation and japa, the more thrilled I am to find this book. It is a complete spiritual path of Yoga."—*Arnold Van Wie*

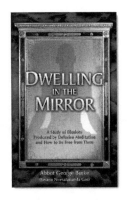

Dwelling in the Mirror
A Study of Illusions Produced by Delusive Meditation and How to Be Free from Them

"There are those who can have an experience and realize that it really cannot be real, but a vagary of their mind. Some may not understand that on their own, but can be shown by others the truth about it. For them and those that may one day be in danger of meditation-produced delusions I have written this brief study." –Abbot George Burke

What Readers say:

"I totally loved this book! After running across many spiritual and self-help books filled with unrealistic promises, this little jewel had the impact of a triple Espresso."— Sandra Carrington-Smith, author of *Housekeeping for the Soul*

The Dhammapada for Awakening

A Commentary on Buddha's Practical Wisdom

The Dhammapada for Awakening brings a refreshing and timely perspective to ancient wisdom and shows seekers of inner peace practical ways to improve their inner lives today.

It explores the Buddha's answers to the urgent questions, such as "How can I find find lasting peace, happiness and fulfillment that seems so elusive?" and "What can I do to avoid many of the miseries big and small that afflict all of us?".

Abbot George illumines the practical wisdom of Buddha in the Dhammapada, and more importantly, and make that makes that teaching relevant to present day spiritual seekers.

What Readers say:

This is a book you'll want to take your time to read and keep as reference to reread. Highly recommended for earnest spiritual aspirants" *–Anna Hourihan, author, editor, and publisher at Vedanta Shores Press*

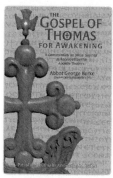

The Gospel of Thomas for Awakening

A Commentary on Jesus' Sayings as Recorded by the Apostle Thomas

"From the very beginning there were two Christianities." So begins this remarkable work. While the rest of the Apostles dispersed to various areas of the Mediterranean world, the apostle Thomas travelled to India, where growing evidence shows that Jesus spent his "Lost Years," and which had been the source of the wisdom which he had brought to the "West."

In *The Gospel of Thomas for Awakening*, Abbot George shines the "Light of the East" on the sometimes enigmatic sayings of Jesus recorded by his apostle Saint Thomas, revealing their unique and rich practical nature for modern day seekers for spiritual life.

What Readers say:

"An extraordinary work of theological commentary, *The Gospel of Thomas for Awakening* is as informed and informative as it is inspired and inspiring".—*James A. Cox, Editor-in-Chief, Midwest Book Review*

The Tao Teh King for Awakening

A Practical Commentary on Lao Tzu's Classic Exposition of Taoism

With penetrating insight, Abbot George Burke illumines the the wisdom of Lao Tzu's classic writing, the Tao Teh King (Tao Te Ching), and the timeless practical value of China's most beloved Taoist scripture for spiritual seekers. With a unique perspective of a lifetime of study and practice of both Eastern and Western spirituality, Abbot George mines the treasures of the Tao Teh King and presents them in an easily intelligible fashion for those wishing to put these priceless teachings into practice.

What Readers say:

"For those who seek spiritual guidance and insight into Lao Tzu's wisdom, this work offers a clear pathway." – *Publisher's Weekly (BookLife Prize)*

The Bhagavad Gita for Awakening

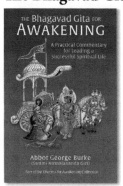

A Practical Commentary for Leading a Successful Spiritual Life

With penetrating insight, Abbot George Burke illumines the Bhagavad Gita's practical value for spiritual seekers. With a unique perspective from a lifetime of study and practice of both Eastern and Western spirituality, Abbot George presents the treasures of the Gita in an easily intelligible fashion.

Drawing from the teachings of Sri Ramakrishna, Jesus, Paramhansa Yogananda, Ramana Maharshi, Swami Vivekananda, Swami Sivananda of Rishikesh, Papa Ramdas, and other spiritual masters and teachers, as well as his own experiences, Abbot Burke illustrates the teachings of the Gita with stories which make the teachings of Krishna in the Gita vibrant and living.

What Readers say:

"This is not a book for only "Hindus" or "Christians." Anyone desiring to better their lives mentally, emotionally, and spiritually would benefit greatly by reading this book."— *Sailaja Kuruvadi*

The Upanishads for Awakening

A Practical Commentary on India's Classical Scriptures

With penetrating insight, Abbot George Burke illumines the Upanishads' practical value for spiritual seekers, and the timelessness of India's most beloved scriptures. With a unique perspective of a lifetime of study and practice of both Eastern and Western spirituality, Abbot George mines the treasures of the Upanishads and presents them in an easily intelligible fashion for those wishing to put these priceless teachings into practice

The teachings of the Upanishads are the supreme expressions of the eternal wisdom, the eternal vision of the ancient rishis (sages) of India. The truths embodied in the Upanishads and their inspired digest-summary, the Bhagavad Gita, are invaluable for all who would ascend to higher consciousness.

What Readers say:

"It is always a delight to see how he seamlessly integrates the wisdom of the West into the East." –*Roopa Subramani*

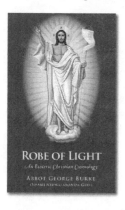

Robe of Light

An Esoteric Christian Cosmology

In *Robe of Light* Abbot George Burke explores the whys and wherefores of the mystery of creation. From the emanation of the worlds from the very Being of God, to the evolution of the souls to their ultimate destiny as perfected Sons of God, the ideal progression of creation is described. Since the rebellion of Lucifer and the fall of Adam and Eve from Paradise flawed the normal plan of evolution, a restoration was necessary. How this came about is the prime subject of this insightful study.

What Readers say:

"Robe of Light actually exceeded my expectations. Abbot Burke explicates the subject perfectly, making a difficult and complex subject like Christian cosmology accessible to those of us who are not great theologians."—*Russ Thomas*

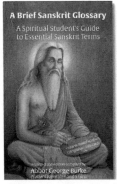

A Brief Sanskrit Glossary
A Spiritual Student's Guide to Essential Sanskrit Terms

This Sanskrit glossary contains full translations and explanations of many of the most commonly used spiritual Sanskrit terms, and will help students of the Bhagavad Gita, the Upanishads, the Yoga Sutras of Patanjali, and other Indian scriptures and philosophical works to expand their vocabularies to include the Sanskrit terms contained in them, and gain a fuller understanding in their studies.

What Readers say:

"If you are reading the writings of Swami Sivananda you will find a basketful of untranslated Sanskrit words which often have no explanation, as he assumes his readers have a background in Hindu philosophy. For writings like his, this book is invaluable, as it lists frequently used Sanskrit terms used in writings on yoga and Hindu philosophical thought.

—*Simeon Davis*

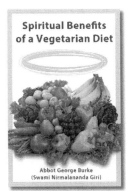

Spiritual Benefits of a Vegetarian Diet

The health benefits of a vegetarian diet are well known, as are the ethical aspects. But the spiritual advantages should be studied by anyone involved in meditation, yoga, or any type of spiritual practice.

Although diet is commonly considered a matter of physical health alone, since the Hermetic principle "as above, so below" is a fundamental truth of the cosmos, diet is a crucial aspect of emotional, intellectual, and spiritual development as well. For diet and consciousness are interrelated, and purity of diet is an effective aid to purity and clarity of consciousness.

A second essay, *Christian Vegetarianism*, continues with a consideration of the esoteric side of diet, the vegetarian roots of early Christianity, and an insightful exploration of vegetarianism in the Old and New Testaments.

Available as a free Kindle ebook download at Amazon.com.

Foundations of Yoga
Ten Important Principles Every Meditator Should Know

An in-depth examination of the important foundation principles of Patanjali's Yoga, Yama & Niyama.

Yama and Niyama are often called the Ten Commandments of Yoga, but they have nothing to do with the ideas of sin and virtue or good and evil as dictated by some cosmic potentate. Rather they are determined on a thoroughly practical, pragmatic basis: that which strengthens and facilitates our yoga practice should be observed and that which weakens or hinders it should be avoided.

It is not a matter of being good or bad, but of being wise or foolish. Each one of these Five Don'ts (Yama) and Five Do's (Niyama) is a supporting, liberating foundation of Yoga. An introduction to the important foundation principles of Patanjali's Yoga: Yama & Niyama

Available as a free Kindle ebook download at Amazon.com, as well as in paperback.

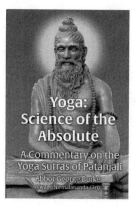

Yoga: Science of the Absolute
A Commentary on the Yoga Sutras of Patanjali

In Yoga: Science of the Absolute, Abbot George Burke draws on the age-long tradition regarding this essential text, including the commentaries of Vyasa and Shankara, the most highly regarded writers on Indian philosophy and practice, as well as I. K. Taimni and other authoritative commentators, and adds his own ideas based on half a century of study and practice. Serious students of yoga will find this an essential addition to their spiritual studies.

What Readers say:

"Abbot George has provided a commentary that is not only deeply informative, making brilliant connections across multiple traditions, but eminently practical. More importantly he describes how they can help one empower their own practice, their own sadhana." —Michael Sabani

May a Christian Believe in Reincarnation?

Discover the real and surprising history of reincarnation and Christianity.

A growing number of people are open to the subject of past lives, and the belief in rebirth—reincarnation, metempsychosis, or transmigration—is becoming commonplace. It often thought that belief in reincarnation and Christianity are incompatible. But is this really true? May a Christian believe in reincarnation? The answer may surprise you.

Reincarnation-also known as the transmigration of souls-is not just some exotic idea of non-Christian mysticism. Nor is it an exclusively Hindu-Buddhist teaching.

In orthodox Jewish and early Christian writings, as well as the Holy Scriptures, we find reincarnation as a fully developed belief, although today it is commonly ignored. But from the beginning it has been an integral part of Orthodox Judaism, and therefore as Orthodox Jews, Jesus and his Apostles would have believed in rebirth.

What Readers say:

"Those needing evidence that a belief in reincarnation is in accordance with teachings of the Christ need look no further: Plainly laid out and explained in an intelligent manner from one who has spent his life on a Christ-like path of renunciation and prayer/meditation."—*Christopher T. Cook*

Coming Soon

The Odes of Solomon: A Commentary

The Aquarian Gospel for Awakening

Notes

Made in the USA
Middletown, DE
01 February 2024

48962181R00083